TOUCH
AND
FLAG FOOTBALL

TOUCH AND

FLAG FOOTBALL

A Guide
for
Players
and
Officials

LOUIS M. MARCIANI

South Brunswick and New York: A. S. Barnes and Company
London: Thomas Yoseloff Ltd

A. S. Barnes and Co., Inc.
Cranbury, New Jersey 08512

Thomas Yoseloff Ltd
108 New Bond Street
London W1Y OQX, England

Library of Congress Cataloging in Publication Data

Marciani, Louis M   1945-
  Touch and flag football.

  Bibliography: p.
  Includes index.
  1. Touch football. I. Title.
GV952.M37   796.33'28   74-9290
ISBN 0-498-01513-0

PRINTED IN THE UNITED STATES OF AMERICA

Contents

Preface   7
Acknowledgments   9

1 General Comments   13
2 Pregame Activities   23
3 Officials' Jurisdiction and Responsibilities   30
4 Game Situations and Officials' Responsibilities   34
5 Cartooned Rule Illustrations   101
6 Officials' Self-Analysis   159
7 Summary of Penalties   169
8 Official Code of Signals   171

Bibliography   183
Index   185

Preface

Touch and flag football leagues are an integral part of competitive recreation programs throughout the United States. Administrators of these programs, no matter whether they are educational, community recreation, or military, all face one basic problem in regard to these leagues: the proper training of touch and flag football officials.

Each program utilizes various combinations of printed material and visual aids to train its officials. Many of the aids used in an illustrative capacity are quite cumbersome (i.e., films, overhead transparencies) and can only be used in group clinic sessions. There was a definite need for a more practical illustrative approach to the training of touch and flag football officials. Thus came the basis for the development of this cartooned officials' guide.

This guide has been developed to serve as a supplementary device to be used in conjunction with the *Official National Touch and Flag Football Rules*. It offers a quick and easy way to learn the mechanics of officiating and at the same time presents a simplified approach to the understanding of the official rules.

The guide consists of simplified cartooned illustrations of actual officiating situations with emphasis on position and duties of three- and two-man officiating crews, the officials pregame activities, jurisdiction and responsibilities, and the officials' code of signals with captions explaining the illustrations. Since many leagues assign only two officials, this guide will emphasize the responsibilities and duties of the two-man crew.

The guide is divided into eight parts. The first part provides general comments on officiating. The second part details the pregame responsibilities of the officials.

The third part presents the overall jurisdictions and responsibilities of the entire officiating crew, while the fourth part presents the specific positions and duties of each official.

The fifth part gives the prospective official an easy and simplified means of understanding the *Official National Touch and Flag Football Rules* and their application.

The sixth part looks at the most frequent rule questions asked by officials in touch and flag football.

The seventh part presents a summary of the penalties for touch and flag football infractions, and in the eighth part the officials' code of signals is presented in an easy learning format.

It is my hope that this guide may serve as a valuable aid to the individual in his understanding of the mechanics of officiating and the *Official National Touch and Flat Football Rules*. Furthermore, it is hoped that this guide can be integrated into formalized programs of study in such areas as intramural administration, organization and leadership of recreation, and sports officiating courses. Many of the officiating chapters, associations, and leagues in the country can also benefit greatly from the utilization of this guide to assist those who are assigned to officiate touch and flag football contests. Many coaches, players, and spectators may also find this guide helpful in obtaining a clearer understanding of touch and flag football.

Acknowledgments

I would like to gratefully acknowledge the time and efforts of many people who helped make *Touch and Flag Football: A Guide for Players And Officials* a reality.

Mr. Dick Grapes of the Western New York Football Officials Association, who provided patience, encouragment, and technical wisdom. A real special thanks to Mike Ricigiliano who contributed the numerous cartooned illustrations.

I want to acknowledge the State University of New York Faculty Grant for the Improvement of Undergraduate Instruction for providing the funds to complete the book, and also for the opportunity of following, in general, the Official National Touch and Flag Football Rules in the compilation of this book.

TOUCH
AND
FLAG FOOTBALL

1

General Comments

This guide consists of simplified, cartooned illustrations of actual officiating situations with emphasis on position and duties of three- and two-man officiating crews, the officials pregame activities, jurisdiction and responsibilities, and the officials' code of signals with captions explaining the illustrations.

The use of a three-man crew—the referee, umpire, and linesman—is recommended. Since many leagues assign only two officials (the referee and linesman), this guide will also emphasize the responsibilities and duties of the two-man crew.

The recommended procedures for the two systems are correlated so that it is possible to adjust easily and efficiently from one system to the other.

The three-man officiating crew consists of

| Umpire | Referee | Linesman |

The two-man officiating crew consists of

Referee   Linesman

KNOWLEDGE OF THE RULES

The first prerequisite of any official is a perfect understanding of the rules and their application. Of course, this alone is not enough to make one a qualified official because there are other attributes that are of equal importance. In addition to complete mastery of the rules, officials must have a good knowledge of human nature and the ability to control situations as they arise. All officials must possess a combination of these if they are to successfully perform their duties properly.

Each official shares an equal responsibility for rule interpretation. Constant study and review of the rule book and guide are necessary in order to perform your job effectively. It is expected that each official will exercise good judgment in applying the rules. The officials should have complete understanding of the letter as well as the spirit of the rules, and administer them consistently and fairly.

KNOWLEDGE OF
THE OFFICIATING PROCEDURE

Each official in the crew is equally responsible for any mistakes in the officiating mechanics as outlined in this guide. It is very important for each official to know not only his position on the playing field, but also the positions of the other officials. At any moment he may be required to assume the duties of a fellow official who is temporarily out of position in the course of covering a play. He is required to have a good working knowledge of the duties of the other officials as well.

This guide will not instruct officials on how to make instant decisions, show poise, control temper, or be firm with their decisions; but officials who are positioned properly and are working the game alertly find that the tangible requirements of good officiating follow naturally.

USE OF SIGNALS

It is very important for all the officials to use the correct officials' signals. This is important to aid in communication with the coaches, players, fellow officials, and spectators. This important aspect of officiating is the only means through which decisions can be relayed. Unauthorized and improper execution of signals does nothing but confuse the situation.

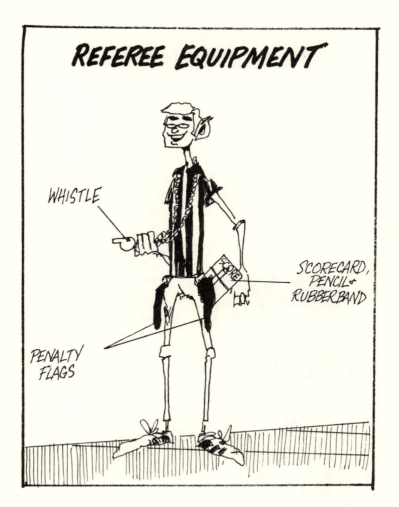

All officials must appear neat. The officials' uniform and equipment consist of:

1. Black and white vertically striped shirt. All officials in a given game are to wear the same type shirt.
2. Whistle.
3. Penalty flag with a clip or small weight attached.
4. Game card with pencil and rubber bands to keep track of the number of downs.

   NOTE: The umpire has the stopwatch to keep game time.

SOUNDING WHISTLE

Sounding the whistle sharply contributes to a reduction of fouls. The official who is covering the runner is primarily responsible for sounding the whistle when the ball becomes dead and indicating this by extending his hand at arm's length above his head.

Find the ball before sounding the whistle. Officials can avoid inadvertently sounding their whistle if they carry them in their hands rather than their mouths.

If a whistle is sounded inadvertently the ball becomes dead immediately.

If this occurs during a kick or while a forward pass is in flight, the play will be replayed.

If it occurs at any other time, even while the ball is not in the player's possession, the officials must determine where the ball was when the whistle sounded. The ball will be put into play for the next down from that spot.

Each official will refrain from using his whistle until he actually sees the ball in possession of a runner who is down or whose forward progress is stopped. If you follow these easy steps, an early whistle will not occur.

When the officials are positioned properly and are cooperating, they can keep the ball in view at all times. Player safety is the official's first responsibility at all times. The official should move in quickly and see that all action stops on the whistle.

OFFICIALS' TIPS

All officiating positions are of equal importance.

As given in the rule book and the officials' guide, all officials should assume their correct positions.

Each official should carry out his primary responsibilities first and then assist in those areas where concurrent responsibilities lie.

It is the crew responsibility to remember the sequence of plays in every series of downs.

Do not miss a down. All officials should check on the down and the distance to be gained on all plays.

All officials must work together. If a rule has been interpreted incorrectly, take a referee's time-out to discuss it.

All officials must be calm, because football is an emotional game and may possibly excite the players.

Try to prevent argument or fights.

Abusive or foul language directed by a coach or player to another player or official must be stopped immediately.

You can see more from farther out. Therefore, do not get too close to the play.

Call rule infractions immediately.

When calling a penalty, do not overemphasize the call.

All officials should be firm and maintain discipline at all times.

All officials should know who the captains are.

The officials should recognize a time-out request from the field captain only.

Each official should record all team time-outs.

Do not blow your whistle on anticipation.

All signals by the officials should be deliberate and distinct at all times.

Each official should call what he sees and remember to be cool, collected, and courteous.

Each official should be sure of a foul he calls. Never guess.

All officials should be in position to call fouls. Call fouls only in your territory unless other officials are not in position to see.

All officials should not seek fouls or hunt for trouble.

2

Pregame Activities

PREGAME CONFERENCE

The entire crew should arrive on the field at least ten minutes prior to the game. The first responsibility should be an officials' conference.

All officials should attend the pregame conference. The referee is responsible for conducting this conference. Below is an agenda that should be followed:

1. Check equipment—whistles, game cards, stopwatch, downmarkers.
2. Review and discuss pertinent rules and interpretations.
3. Review and discuss the following mechanics:
   - Methods of spotting the ball.
   - Position and responsibilities on:
     a. Free kicks
     b. Running plays
     c. Passing plays
     d. Scrimmage kicks
     e. Extra-point attempts and field goals
     f. First downs
     g. Time-outs.
4. Discuss procedure for calling fouls and exacting penalties.

Following the pregame conference, the officials will proceed and perform the pregame duties.

PREGAME DUTIES OF OFFICIALS

Each member of the crew has a number of important duties to perform prior to the start of the game.

R E F E R E E

The Referee's duties consist of:
1. Securing the game ball.
2. Inspecting the playing field.
3. Informing both captains of the starting time.

L I N E S M A N

The linesman's duties consist of:
1. Securing and checking the down marker.
2. Obtaining the home captain for the pregame toss.

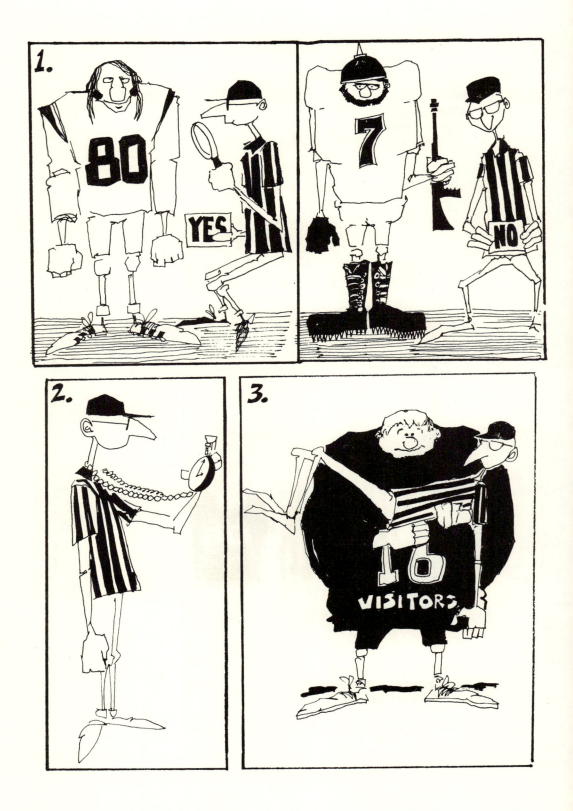

U M P I R E

The umpire's duties consist of:
1. Checking player equipment.
2. Checking game watch.
3. Obtaining the visiting captain for the pregame toss.

THE COIN TOSS

About three minutes prior to the start of the game, the captains of the respective teams will be escorted to the center of the field. The linesman will escort the home captain, and the visiting captain will be escorted by the umpire. The referee will introduce the captains and give them their instructions.

The referee will instruct the visiting captain to call heads or tails while the coin is in the air.

The referee will then indicate the winner by placing a hand on his shoulder and asking him to choose whether he will kick or receive, or whether he will choose the goal he will defend.

After this choice has been made, the loser of the toss will make his choice.

The referee instructs the captains to face each other, with each facing in the direction of the goal toward which his team will be attempting to advance.

The referee should then face in the same direction as the winner of the toss and simulate his choice with either a kicking or a catching motion.

This should be followed by facing in the other direction and simulating the loser's choice.

At the completion of the toss procedure, the referee dismisses the captains. All officials should record which team has the first choice for the second half.

3

Officials' Jurisdiction and Duties

It is the responsibility of every official to know precisely where he should be, what he should observe, and how to cooperate with his fellow officials on every play situation.

An official who is in the right position at the right time and observing the play in the correct direction will have a better chance of making the correct decision when necessary.

OFFICIALS' JURISDICTION AND DUTIES

This officials' guide is an integral part in the learning process of the officials' job, especially in regard to the specific duties, mechanics, and procedures for each official during any play situation. All play situations with individual official's responsibilities are detailed position by position in the subsequent part. The general duties of each official shall be given in this part. The jurisdiction and duties will vary with the number of officials refereeing the game. While the *Official National Touch and Flag Football Rules* recommend a three- or four-man officiating team, I am well aware of the fact that many leagues assign only two officials to a contest. With this in mind, the jurisdiction and duties of a three- and two-man crew will be presented.

GENERAL OFFICIALS' RESPONSIBILITIES

1. All officials are responsible for any decision involving the application, interpretation, or enforcement of a rule.

2. If an official errs in his interpretation of a rule, the other officials must check him before the play is resumed. Otherwise they are equally responsible.
3. In the event of a disagreement, the crew should step aside for a conference (referee's time out).
4. In the event of a crew conference, a majority opinion prevails and the referee's decision on any point in the rules is to be made on such a basis.
5. All officials have concurrent jurisdiction over any foul, and there is no fixed territorial division in this respect. When an official signals a foul, he must report it to the referee, informing him of its nature, the position of the ball at the time of the foul, the offenders (when known), the penalty, and the spot of enforcement.
6. All officials shall record all charged team time-outs during the game, winner of the toss, and the score.
7. Ten minutes prior to game time, the entire crew is to appear on the field and proceed with pregame activities.
8. During any running play (including runbacks) the nearest official is to cover and remain with the ball or the runner.

GENERAL POSITION RESPONSIBILITIES

Each official has definite responsibilities. These specific duties will be covered in the next section. The following responsibilities are in general terms but are essential for specified position.

3 - MAN CREW

Referee
- The referee is to have general control of the game. He has the final authority for the score and number of a down in case of any disagreement.
- His decisions are final except in those matters specifically under the jurisdiction of other officials.
- The referee is to spot the ball where play is to resume.
- After a foul, the referee must announce the penalty to both captains the decision and distance when the enforcement is entirely automatic and there is obviously no choice.
- Prior to plays from scrimmage, the referee's normal position is behind and to the side of the offensive backfield.
- The referee should favor the right or left side according to which arm the passer uses.
- The referee is primarily responsible for spotting the ball at the inbounds spot on plays from scrimmage.
- During time-in when the ball is dead near the sideline, the referee is not to assist in relay to inbounds spot, unless the umpire or linesman has been delayed in doing so.

Umpire

- The umpire shall check equipment.
- The umpire is in charge of timing the game.
- He should assist in relaying the ball to the inbounds spot and previous spot after an incompletion, and the spot of free kick when indicated.
- On plays from scrimmage, the umpire is particularly responsible for observing line play, but he must also cover play that develops after the linemen make their initial charge.
- The umpire should drift downfield to cover a passing play.
- Try to assist the referee on forward and backward passes behind the line.
- Watch for illegal use of hands whenever possible.
- Check with the referee on distance penalties for proper distance and spot of enforcement.
- Never signal for a touchdown unless you actually see the ball in possession cross the plane of the goal line.
- On scrimmage kicks go downfield and keep the potential receiver in view.
- Always remain in position to see the ball and all interior linemen.
- The umpire is responsible for short passes up the middle.

Linesman

- The linesman operates on the side of the field designated by the referee.
- The linesman is responsible over the neutral zone and infractions of the scrimmage formation. He is primarily responsible for offside, encroachment, and action pertaining to the scrimmage line prior to or at the snap.
- The linesman is responsible for the operation of the down marker.
- The linesman must check with the referee as to the number of each down that is about to start.
- The linesman is to mark the out-of-bounds spot on his side of the field when within his range.
- Keep the neutral zone clear.
- After a penalty be sure to double check the down and distance with the referee.
- Unless confined by your sideline, never be closer than five yards to the nearest player.
- Signal time-out immediately after any out-of-bounds on your side.
- Cover a runner all the way to the goal line if he comes into your side zone; declare the ball dead and spot it, or hold it for a toss when required.
- When the play does not enter your side zone, move downfield with the progress. On plays wide away from your side, drift downfield, alert to pick up the runner if he cuts to your side. Indicate progress with out-thrust foot.
- When the play does not enter your side zone, move downfield with the progress. On plays wide from your side, drift downfield watching players, alert to pick up the runner if he cuts to your side. Indicate progress with out-thrust foot.
- On scrimmage kicks, the linesman will drift downfield, observing action involving the receiving team players. Watch for clips. Be alert to pick up the runner.

- On scrimmage kicks, the linesman will drift downfield, observing the action involving the receiving team. Watch for clips.

2 - Man Crew

Referee

- The referee is to have general control of the game. He has the final authority for the score and the number of a down in case of any disagreement.
- The referee's decisions are final except in those matters specifically under the jurisdiction of other officials.
- The referee is to spot the ball where play is to resume.
- On plays from scrimmage, he will take a position straddling the neutral zone five to ten yards from the nearest player.
- On plays from scrimmage, the referee is responsible for the action in the offensive backfield, but he must also cover play that develops after the linemen make their initial charge.
- The referee should drift downfield to cover passing plays.
- After a foul, he must announce the penalty to both captains and explain to the offended captain the decision and choice, as well as the number of the next down and distance.
- It is not imperative to explain to both captains the decision and distance when enforcement is entirely automatic and there is obviously no choice.
- On scrimmage kicks, he will cover the runback to his side.

Linesman

- The linesman operates on the side of the field opposite the referee.
- The linesman is responsible over the neutral zone and infractions of the scrimmage formation. He is responsible for offside, encroachment, and any action pertaining to the scrimmage line prior to or at the snap.
- In addition to watching the line play, he is responsible for the action in the secondary.
- The linesman should drift downfield to cover a passing play.
- The linesman is responsible for the operation of the down marker.
- Before the start of each play, the linesman must check with the referee as to the number of each down.
- He is to mark the out-of-bounds spot on his side of the field when within his range.
- He must keep the neutral zone clear.
- He must double check down and distance with the referee after each play.
- Unless confined by sideline, he should never be closer than five yards to the nearest player.
- He is responsible for keeping time during the game.
- He must signal time-out immediately after any out-of-bounds on his side.
- He must cover the runner all the way to the goal line if the runner comes in his side zone; he must declare the ball dead, spot it, or hold for the toss when required.

4

Game Situations
and Officials'
Responsibilities

Competence in officiating is based on a thorough knowledge of the techniques and mechanics of officiating. It is therefore necessary that all officials know the various duties for all game situations.

Knowing your responsibilities and those of your fellow officials will provide a solid base for the performance of your duties. This, coupled with hard work and a sense for good positioning, should put you on the right track toward good officiating.

CODE OF DIAGRAMS

● *OFFENSE*

○ *DEFENSE*

THREE-MAN OFFICIATING CREW:
POSITIONS AND DUTIES ON KICKOFF

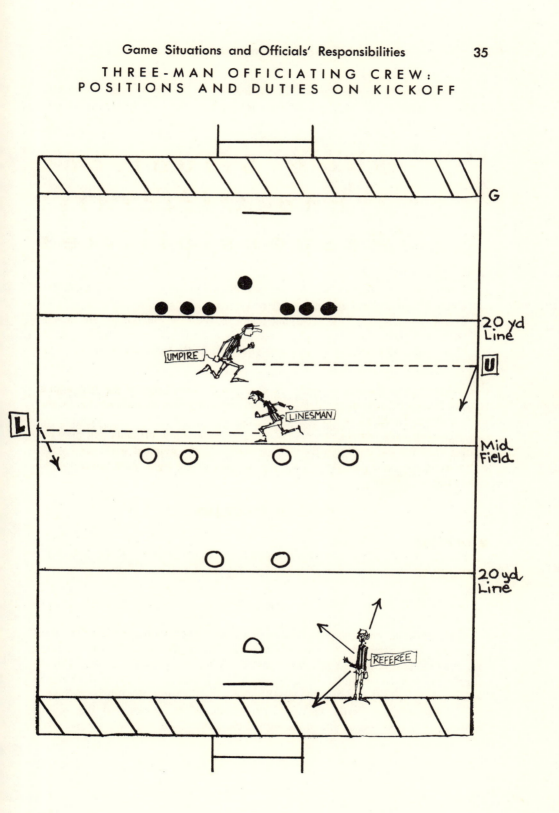

GENERAL

All officials will assume the position as designated by the diagram. After having assumed your positions, all officials (except the referee) should signal with one hand aloft that they are ready for play to start at the referee's signal.

PRIOR TO KICKOFF

Referee

The referee should basically perform three activities prior to the kickoff:
1. Hold arm aloft to request ready signal from the other officials.
2. Motion the umpire and linesman to the sideline.
3. When ready signals have been given, drop your arm and sound your whistle.

Linesman

The linesman should basically perform three activities prior to the kickoff:
1. Upon signal from the referee, move to sideline.
2. Count the players of the receiving team and note whether there are at least three men within five yards of the receiving team's restraining line.
3. Hold your hand aloft to indicate that your side of the field is ready.

Umpire

The umpire should basically perform three activities prior to the kickoff:
1. Count the kicking team players.
2. Get captain's ready signal and instruct the kicker to wait for the referee's signal.
3. On the signal from the referee, move to the sideline on the side opposite that of the linesman and on kicking team's free-kick line.

POSITIONS AND DUTIES ON THE KICKOFF
THREE OFFICIALS

AT AND AFTER THE KICKOFF

At the kick, move into a position that permits you to see the ball and keep the sideline in view at all times. If the kick is caught and advanced, or if a fumble occurs, the nearest official should cover the runner until the ball is dead. Signal the referee instantly. If he is not covering and if the ball is dead in the side zone, pass to the spotter, who will protect the ball until the referee arrives.

While waiting for the kickoff, officials should be thinking of the various situations that may occur at and during the kickoff.

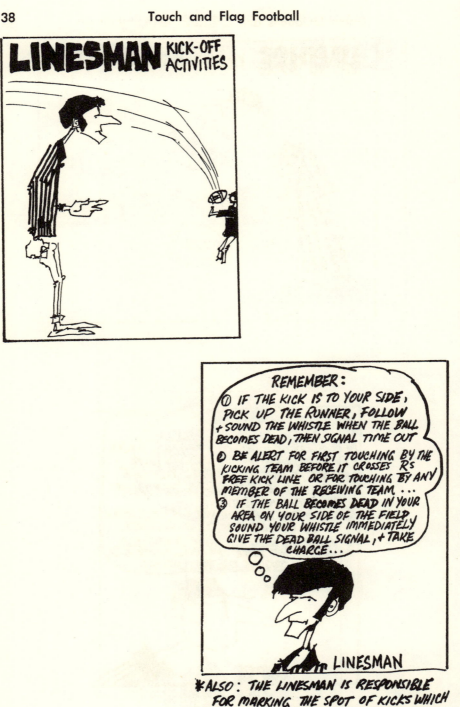

POSITIONS AND DUTIES
ON SCRIMMAGE RUNS

GENERAL

Perform your normal duties up to time of the snap. Each play should be properly boxed in at all times. Each official should widen his position if a spread formation is used.

PRIOR TO THE SCRIMMAGE RUN

Referee

The referee should take the following position prior to the scrimmage run:

After spotting the ball, announce the number of the down and the distance to go. Move away and give the ready-for-play signal accompanied by a short blast on your whistle.

Move to a position in the back of the offensive team on the side opposite the linesman (see diagram).

Linesman

The linesman should take the following position prior to the scrimmage run:

Assume position to fit the formation being used. It will usually be five to ten yards outside the defensive end. It will always be outside of all players in a spread formation, even if it puts you on the sideline (see diagram).

Umpire

The umpire should take the following position prior to the scrimmage run:

Assume a position that is appropriate to the situation. It will probably be fifteen yards behind the defensive line between the defensive ends and on the side opposite the linesman (see diagram).

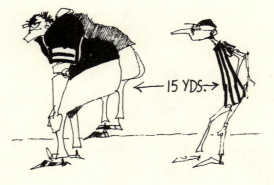

AT AND AFTER THE SCRIMMAGE RUN

Specific duties and activities at and after the scrimmage run are indicated below.

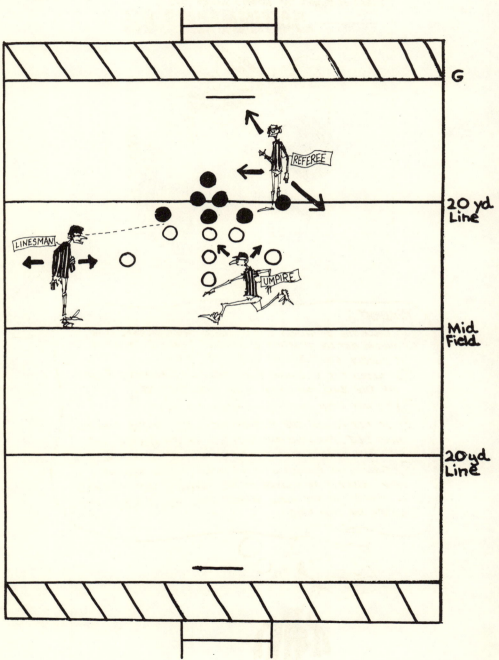

REMEMBER :

① CHECK THE 25 SECOND COUNT, ILLEGAL SHIFT, ILLEGAL SNAP, + MAN in MOTION TOWARD THE OPPOSITE SIDELINE TO SEE HE IS CLEARLY GOING BACKWARDS AT THE SNAP.....

② WATCH THE LINESMAN FOR A SIGNAL ON FOREMOST POINT OF THE BALL ON QUICK PLAYS INTO THE LINE.

③ DO NOT RUSH IN TOO SOON AFTER THE SNAP.

④ DO NOT FOLLOW THE RUNNER TOO CLOSELY TO THE LINESMAN'S SIDE, THE LINESMAN WILL PICK UP THE RUNNER, DECLARE BALL DEAD + TOSS IT BACK TO YOU OR THE UMPIRE

⑤ FOLLOW THE RUNNER ON YOUR SIDE + IF BALL BECOMES DEAD, RELAY IT TO UMPIRE AT THE INBOUNDS SPOT. IF A FOUL IS CALLED I DO NOT BLOW WHISTLE UNTIL BALL IS DEAD. NOTE WHERE THE RUN ENDS.....

POSITIONS AND DUTIES ON RUNNING
PLAY FROM SCRIMMAGE
THREE OFFICIALS

POSITIONS AND DUTIES
ON SCRIMMAGE PASS

GENERAL

The initial position for each official is the same as for a running play from scrimmage. As soon as it is apparent that a passing play is developing, however, each official will adjust slightly to fit the situation (sse diagram).

PRIOR TO SCRIMMAGE PASS

Referee

Observe all backs behind the line of scrimmage to be certain they are legal.

Observe possible contact with the passer.

Watch the passer instead of the flight of the ball.

Be alert to observe any illegal pass and to determine whether the passer is behind the line of scrimmage when he passes the ball.

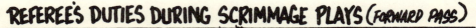

REFEREE'S DUTIES DURING SCRIMMAGE PLAYS (FORWARD PASS)

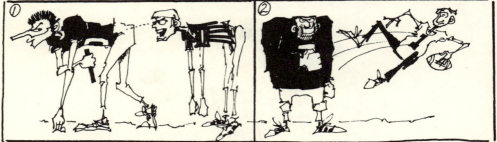

Linesman

Be alert for illegal use of hands and other fouls on the line of scrimmage.

Drift downfield to cover passes on your side.

Umpire

Cover short passes down the middle.

Assist the referee in determining whether the passer was behind the scrimmage line when the ball left his hand.

AT AND AFTER THE SCRIMMAGE PASS

Specific duties and activities at and after the scrimmage pass are indicated below.

ITS IMPORTANT TO REMEMBER :

① WATCH THE PASSER INSTEAD OF THE FLIGHT OF THE BALL

② BE ALERT TO OBSERVE ANY ILLEGAL PASS AND TO DETERMINE WHETHER THE PASSER IS BEHIND THE LINE OF SCRIMMAGE WHEN HE PASSES THE LINE

LINESMAN ACTIVITIES ON A FORWARD PASS

SWOOSH

THINGS TO REMEMBER :

① WATCH FOR INTERFERENCE BY EITHER TEAM AND BE READY TO RULE ON A POSSIBLE FUMBLE OR ILLEGAL PASS AFTER THE PASS IS CAUGHT.

② BE READY TO CHANGE YOUR MOVEMENT IF THE PROSPECTIVE PASSER DECIDES TO RUN....

③ IF THE PASS IS INCOMPLETE, SOUND YOUR WHISTLE, STOP THE CLOCK, AND GIVE THE INCOMPLETE PASS SIGNAL.

④ ON INCOMPLETE PASSES IN YOUR AREA, RELAY THE BALL TO THE UMPIRE.

⑤ IF THE UMPIRE RETRIEVES THE BALL, HELP HIM RELAY IT TO THE REFEREE BY GOING ABOUT HALF THE DISTANCE BETWEEN THE TWO OFFICIALS.

POSITIONS AND DUTIES ON PASSING PLAY FROM SCRIMMAGE: THREE OFFICIALS

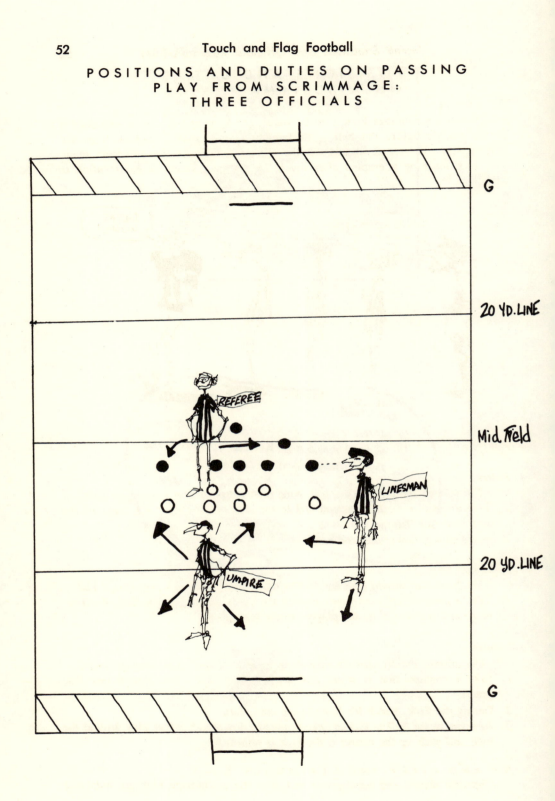

POSITIONS AND DUTIES
ON A SCRIMMAGE KICK

GENERAL

When a scrimmage kick is to be made, the kicking team must announce it to the referee before the ball is declared ready for play. After such an announcement, the referee should tell the other officials and the defensive team. The kick must be attempted after the kicking team announces its intention to kick.

PRIOR TO THE SCRIMMAGE KICK

Referee

The referee should take the following position prior to a scrimmage kick:
1. Take a position slightly behind and to the side of the kicker and opposite the linesman (see diagram).
2. Move slowly down after the kick.

Linesman

The linesman should take the following position prior to a scrimmage kick:
1. Take a position approximately five to ten yards parallel to the line of scrimmage and outside of all the players in the formation.

Umpire

The umpire should take the following position prior to a scrimmage kick:
1. Take a position that is wider and deeper than your usual station (see diagram).
2. During the kick, watch for fouls in the secondary.
3. As soon as the ball is kicked, move quickly downfield, cover play around the ball, and pick up the runner if the kick is returned.

AT AND AFTER THE SCRIMMAGE KICK

Specific duties and activities at and after the scrimmage kick are indicated

POSITION AND DUTIES DURING A KICK FROM SCRIMMAGE: THREE OFFICIALS

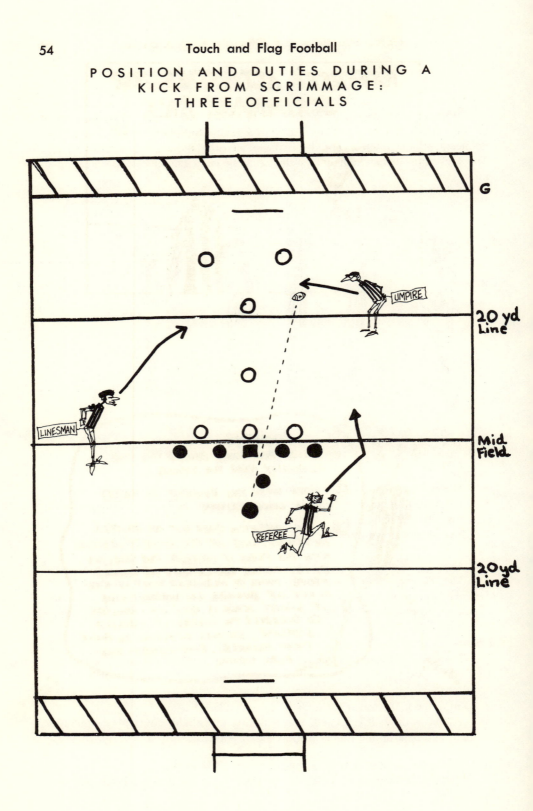

REMEMBER :

① WATCH FOR FOULS BEHIND THE LINE, ESPECIALLY NEAR THE KICKER ...

② MOVE WITH THE RUNNER IF THERE IS A LONG RETURN.

③ IF A LONG KICK GOES OUT OF BOUNDS IN FLIGHT, LINE UP THE NEAREST OFFICIAL WITH THE PLACE IT CROSSED THE SIDELINE BY INDICATING WHICH WAY HE SHOULD MOVE. MOVE TO INBOUNDS SPOT IF KICK IS OUT OF BOUNDS ON UMPIRE'S SIDE. IF SHORT KICK IS OUT-OF-BOUNDS, GO DIRECTLY TO WHERE IT CROSSED SIDELINE, SIGNAL OFFICIAL TO MOVE DOWN MARKER, GIVE READY-FOR-PLAY SIGNAL.

REMEMBER :

① IF THE KICK IS FIRST TOUCHED BY "K" DROP A MARKER TO DESIGNATE THE SPOT OF FIRST TOUCHING.

② IF "K" IS THE FIRST TO TOUCH THE KICKED BALL AT REST BEYOND THE LINE, SOUND YOUR WHISTLE IMMEDIATELY.

③ IF THE KICK GOES OUT OF BOUNDS ALONG YOUR SIDELINE, SOUND YOUR WHISTLE, SIGNAL OUT-OF-BOUNDS, HOLD THE SPOT & CONTINUE TO OBSERVE PLAY UNTIL ALL ACTION SUBSIDES.

④ IF THE KICK IS TO THE LINESMAN'S SIDE, MOVE SLOWLY DOWNFIELD WATCHING FOR FOULS IN THE SECONDARY.

⑤ IF THE BALL GOES OUT OF BOUNDS ON THE LINESMAN'S SIDE, MOVE QUICKLY TO THE INBOUNDS SPOT TO RECEIVE A PASS FROM THE LINESMAN & SPOT THE BALL.

POSITIONS AND DUTIES FOR
TRY-FOR-POINT AND FIELD GOAL

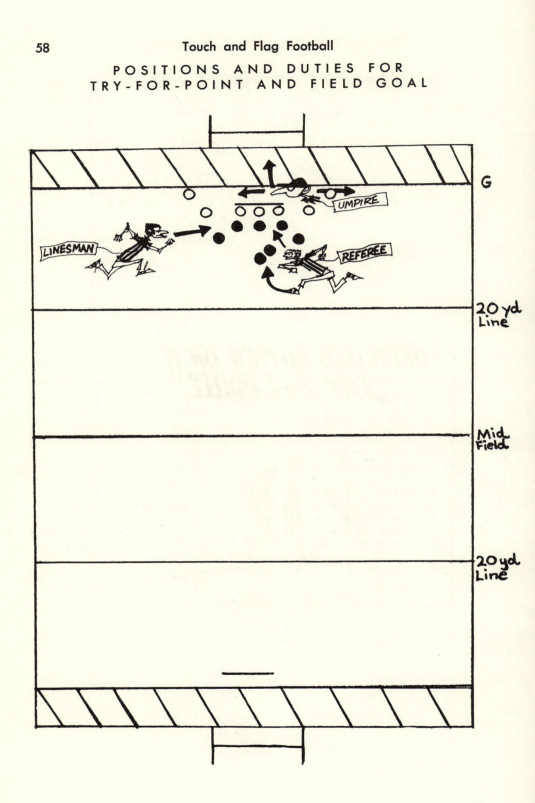

GENERAL

Assume the positions indicated by the diagram. Be alert for a pass or a run. When the try ends, the referee sounds the whistle and signals score or no score (see diagram).

AT AND AFTER TRY-FOR-POINT AND FIELD GOAL

Specific duties and activities at and after try-for-point and field goal are indicated below.

POSITIONS AND DUTIES FOR
TRY-FOR-POINT AND FIELD GOAL:
THREE OFFICIALS

Referee must be behind the kicker to cover acts in his vicinity and to judge whether the kick goes through the goal.

The umpire must be near the goal line to rule whether the ball passes above the crossbar.

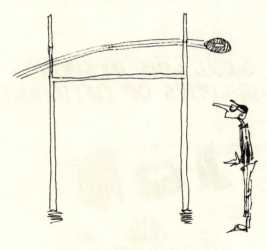

The linesman must watch for roughness against the kicker or the placekick holder.

POSITIONS AND DUTIES FOR
GOAL-LINE PLAYS

GENERAL

Each official must take over specific assignments for accurate and instant rulings. Smooth teamwork is imperative. Assume the positions shown in the field diagram.

AT AND AFTER GOAL-LINE PLAY

Referee

The referee should remember the following:

1. Observe the play on and behind the line.
2. Be alert for a fumble.
3. Avoid following the runner too closely.
4. Do not make a close touchdown decision from behind the runner unless it is obvious that a touchdown has been scored.
5. Give the touchdown signal if a touchdown has been signaled by another official.

Linesman

The linesman should remember the following:

1. Observe action on the line.

2. Be ready to drift quickly into the end zone if a forward pass has been thrown.

3. Be alert to detect the farthest point to which the ball is advanced.

4. If you see the ball (in possession of a runner) touch or cross the goal-line plane, instantly give the touchdown signal.

Umpire

The umpire should remember the following:

1. Take a position near the goal line and opposite the linesman (see field diagram).
2. Concentrate on the player action in the line, and be alert for a forward pass play.
3. For a forward pass play:
   Avoid making a signal if there is doubt about a touchdown.

POSITIONS AND DUTIES
FOR GOAL-LINE PLAYS:
THREE OFFICIALS

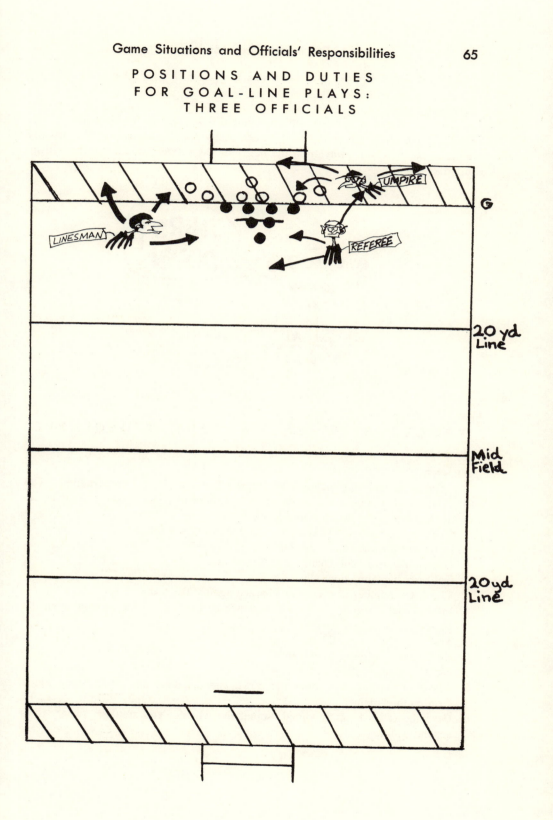

DECLARING THE BALL READY FOR PLAY

Referee

After the ball is spotted and the other officials are in position, the referee should move away promptly and give the ready-for-play signal. This is usually done on the first step away from the ball, and the referee should use the whistle to attract attention.

PROCEDURE WHEN TIME-OUT IS DECLARED

GENERAL

The term *time-out* includes all times when the clock is not running. The time-out signal is given and repeated by the other officials. Make a written record if the time-out is charged to a team.

AT AND AFTER TIME-OUT IS SIGNALED

The referee has the following duties:

1. Use your whistle and clearly signal time-out.
2. Get team captains' approval.
3. Check the number of time-outs charged against the team.
4. Inform each team of the down, distance to gain, and time remaining in the period.
5. Take a position over the ball.
6. Keep time with your own watch.
7. Notify the team after sixty seconds.
8. Move to the ball, announce the down and distance, and get a ready signal from both captains.
9. Give the ready-for-play signal, sound the whistle, and start the twenty-five-second count.

The linesman and umpire have the following duties:

1. Maintain positions near the team huddles. The umpire stays with the defensive unit, and the linesman with the offensive unit.

PROCEDURE FOR PENALTY ADMINISTRATION

GENERAL

When the officials observe a foul, follow this procedure:

1. Drop a marker and continue to observe the play.

2. Note the location of the ball at the time of the foul.

3. As soon as the ball becomes dead after a live-ball foul, signal time-out.

4. Give the preliminary signal. If the umpire or linesman called the foul, tell the referee what it is.

5. The referee will talk with the captains.

6. Walk off the penalty or decline the penalty (referee).

7. Referee: give the foul signal again.

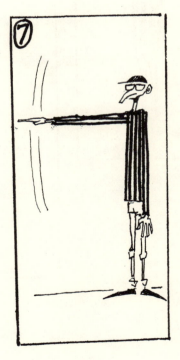

8. Referee: give the ready-for-play signal.

9. The referee will wind the clock.

REFEREE'S DUTIES AS SOON AS THE BALL BECOMES DEAD AFTER THE FOUL

Give the time-out signal and get full information from the official who called the foul. Give the preliminary signal, then call the captain of the offended team and briefly inform him of the down and distance if the penalty were to be accepted. Give the same information if the penalty were to be declined.

GIVE TIME-OUT SIGNAL   PRELIMINARY SIGNAL

YOU CAN TAKE THE DOWN OR YARDAGE   WE'LL TAKE THE YARDAGE

If the captain's most advantageous choice is obvious, the referee will briefly and quickly inform him. This will be only a signal and a brief statement.

If two penalties are to be administered, the proper signals should be given before and after each measurement.

REFEREE WHEN ADMINISTERING PENALTIES

1. Take the ball to the spot of administration.

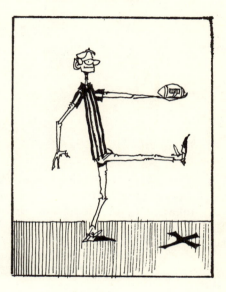

2. If, after the options have been explained, the captain of the offended team accepts the penalty, proceed with enforcement. Spot the ball.

3. Step away and give the proper signal for the foul to both sidelines.

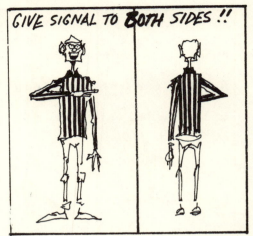

GIVE SIGNAL TO **BOTH** SIDES !!

4. If the penalty is declined, go to the spot of the ball, give the foul signal followed by the declination signal to both sidelines.

5. If there is a double foul, place the ball at the spot for the next down, signal each foul facing each sideline, and follow this with the penalty declined signal.

LINESMAN'S DUTIES AS SOON AS THE BALL BECOMES DEAD AFTER THE FOUL

1. Be ready to move the down marker.
2. Double check the enforcement of the penalty and be certain of the number of the down.

UMPIRE'S DUTIES AS SOON AS THE BALL BECOMES
DEAD AFTER THE FOUL

1. During the administration of all penalties, the umpire shall receive the ball
   and take it to the spot from which the referee will measure the penalty.
2. Hold this spot during administration of the penalty in order to check the yardage assessment.

PROCEDURE FOR DEAD-BALL FOUL

1. Give the dead-ball signal.

2. Give the preliminary signal.

3. Talk to the captains.

4. Walk off the penalty or decline the penalty.

5. Give the foul signal again.

6. Declare the ball ready for play or signal the clock to start, depending upon the act that caused the clock to be stopped.

PROCEDURE AT END OF THE GAME

All officials have certain procedures to follow at the conclusion of the game.

1. Provide for the care of the equipment.

2. The referee should take charge of the game ball at the end of each half and return it to the proper place when the game is over.

3. Do not discuss the game on the field.

4. If there has been any flagrant irregularity, report it as soon as possible to the proper authorities.

TWO-MAN OFFICIATING CREW: POSITIONS AND DUTIES ON THE KICKOFF

GENERAL

Assume the position as designated by the field diagram. After having assumed your position, the linesman should signal with one hand aloft indicating that he is ready for play to start.

PRIOR TO THE KICKOFF

The referee should basically perform the following activities prior to the kick-off:

1. Count the players of the receiving team and note whether there are at least three men within five yards of the receiving team's restraining line.
2. Hold an arm aloft to request the ready signal from the other official.
3. Motion the linesman to the sideline.
4. After the ready signals have been given, drop your arm and sound your whistle.

Linesman

The linesman should basically perform the following activities prior to the kickoff:

1. Count the kicking-team players.
2. Get the captains' ready signal and instruct the kicker to wait for the referee's signal.
3. Upon signal from the referee, move to the sideline opposite that of the referee.
4. Hold your hand aloft indicating that your side of the field is ready.

Referee

While waiting for the kickoff, the referee should be thinking about the following activities:

AT AND AFTER THE KICKOFF

At the kick, move into a position that permits you to see the ball and keep the sideline in view at all times. If the kick is caught and advanced or a fumble occurs, the nearest official should cover the runner until the ball is dead. Signal the referee instantly.

Linesman

While waiting for the kickoff, the linesman should be thinking about the following activities:

- WATCH FOR OFFSIDES VIOLATION BY THE KICKING TEAM
- BE ALERT FOR THE FIRST TOUCHING OF A KICK BY A MEMBER OF THE KICKING TEAM BEFORE IT CROSSES R's FREE KICK LINE OR HAS BEEN TOUCHED BY A MEMBER OF THE RECEIVING TEAM.
- LINESMAN IS RESPONSIBLE FOR MARKING THE SPOT OF KICKS WHICH GO OUT-OF-BOUNDS ON HIS SIDE OF THE FIELD.
- IF BALL BECOMES DEAD IN HIS AREA, THE LINESMAN MUST SOUND HIS WHISTLE IMMEDIATELY, GIVE THE DEAD BALL SIGNAL.
- AFTER THE BALL HAS BEEN LEGALLY TOUCHED THE LINESMAN MUST START HIS WATCH.
- AS THE BALL TRAVELS DOWN FIELD, THE LINESMAN MUST MOVE IN THAT DIRECTION WHILE WATCHING FOR FOULS + TOUCHING OF THE BALL CARRIER.
- UPON RECEIVING THE APPROPRIATE SIGNAL FROM THE REFEREE, MOVE THE DOWN MARKER TO A POINT PERPENDICULAR TO THE FORWARD MOST PT. OF THE BALL.

POSITIONS AND DUTIES ON THE KICKOFF

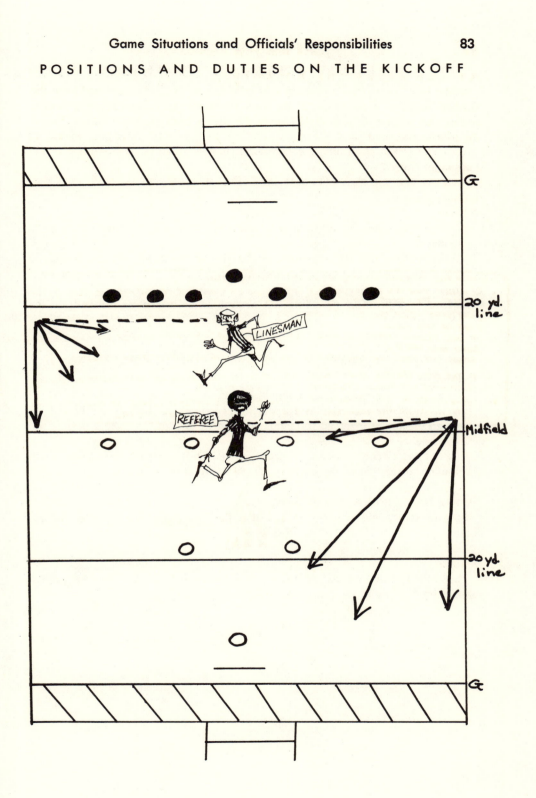

POSITIONS AND DUTIES
ON SCRIMMAGE RUNS

GENERAL

Perform your normal duties up to the time of the snap. Each play should be properly boxed in at all times. Each official should widen his position if a spread formation is used.

PRIOR TO THE SCRIMMAGE RUN

Referee

The referee should perform the following activities prior to a play from scrimmage:

1. After spotting the ball, announce the number of the down and the distance to go. Move away and give the ready-for-play signal accompanied by a short blast of the whistle.
2. Move to a position straddling the neutral zone five to ten yards from the nearest player.

Linesman

The linesman should perform the following activities prior to a play from scrimmage:

1. The linesman's field position should be straddling the neutral zone five to ten yards from the nearest player opposite the referee. It will always be outside of all players in a spread formation, even if he is forced to take a position on the sideline.
2. Check the twenty-five-second count, illegal shift, illegal snap, and man in motion to see that he is clearly going backward at the snap.

AT AND AFTER THE SCRIMMAGE RUN

Specific duties and activities at and after the scrimmage run are indicated below.

Referee

While waiting for the offensive team to break their huddle, the referee should be thinking of the following possibilities:

- CHECK ON INTERFERENCE WITH THE SNAP & FALSE STARTS BY THE OFFENSE
- AFTER THE SNAP, DO NOT COVER THE BALL CLOSELY, BUT CHECK ON ILLEGAL USE OF HANDS & OTHER FOULS NEAR THE LINE OF SCRIMMAGE.
- DO NOT FOLLOW THE RUNNER TOO CLOSELY ON A RUN TO LINESMAN'S SIDE OF THE FIELD. THE LINESMAN WILL PICK UP RUNNER IN HIS AREA, DECLARE BALL DEAD, & TOSS IT BACK TO REFEREE AT THE APPROPRIATE INBOUNDS SPOT.
- ON RUN TO REFEREE'S SIDE, PICK UP RUNNER & IF THE BALL BECOMES DEAD IN THE SIDE ZONE, HE MUST RELAY IT TO THE LINESMAN AT THE INBOUNDS SPOT. THE REFEREE MUST ALSO BE COGNIZANT OF NOTING WHERE RUNS TO HIS SIDE OF THE FIELD SO THAT HE MAY MARK THE BALL'S POSITION ACCURATELY FOR THE NEXT DOWN.
- IF THE OFF. TEAM IS DOING A GREAT DEAL OF PASSING, IT IS THE REFEREE'S OPTION TO ADJUST HIS POSITION.
- WATCH FOR FOULS IN THE SECONDARY
  - ON A PASS PLAY, NOTE WHETHER THE PASS GOES BEYOND THE LINE OF SCRIMMAGE.
  - SIGNAL THE LINESMAN TO MOVE THE DOWN MARKERS IF NO PENALTY HAS OCCURRED OR AFTER THE APPROPRIATE PENALTY YARDAGE HAS BEEN ASSESSED.

REFEREE

Touch and Flag Football

Linesman

While waiting for the offensive play to begin, the linesman should be thinking about the following activities:

- WATCH FOR ENCROACHMENT, OFFSIDES, FALSE STARTS, + ILLEGAL USE OF HANDS
- ASSIST REFEREE IN DETERMINING FOREMOST PROGRESS OF THE BALL. SIGNAL HIM WITH ONE FOOT THRUST FORWARD
- THE LINESMAN MUST NEVER TURN HIS BACK ON THE RUNNER.
- IF A WIDE RUN DEVELOPS TO THE LINESMAN'S SIDE + HE IS UNABLE TO RETREAT FAST ENOUGH TO STAY OUTSIDE OF THE PLAY + HE SHOULD COMPENSATE BY FADING TOWARD THE OFFENSIVE TEAM'S HALF OF THE FIELD + THEN FOLLOW THE MAN DOWNFIELD.
- WHEN MOVING WITH THE RUNNER, BE ALERT FOR AN ILLEGAL FORWARD PASS OR A FUMBLE.
- KNOW THE SPOT OF THE PASS OR FUMBLE + THE SPOT OF ANY SUBSEQUENT FOUL.
- WHEN BALL COMES TO LINESMAN'S SIDE OF THE FIELD, HE SHOULD MOVE WITH IT, + WHEN IT BECOMES DEAD, MOVE IN, SOUND WHISTLE + SPOT THE BALL.
- WHEN BALL BECOMES DEAD IN THE LINESMAN'S SIDE ZONE, HE MUST SPOT THE POINT + THEN PASS IT TO THE REFEREE AT THE CORRESPONDING INBOUNDS SPOT.
- LINESMAN MUST MOVE THE DOWN MARKER TO A POSITION WHICH IS IN A STRAIGHT LINE PERPENDICULAR TO THE FORWARD MOST POINT OF THE BALL AFTER EVERY PLAY FROM SCRIMMAGE PROVIDED A PENALTY HAS NOT OCCURRED, OR, IF A PENALTY HAS OCCURRED AFTER THE APPROPRIATE PENALTY YARDAGE HAS BEEN ASSESSED.

LINESMAN

POSITIONS AND DUTIES ON
RUNNING PLAY FROM SCRIMMAGE

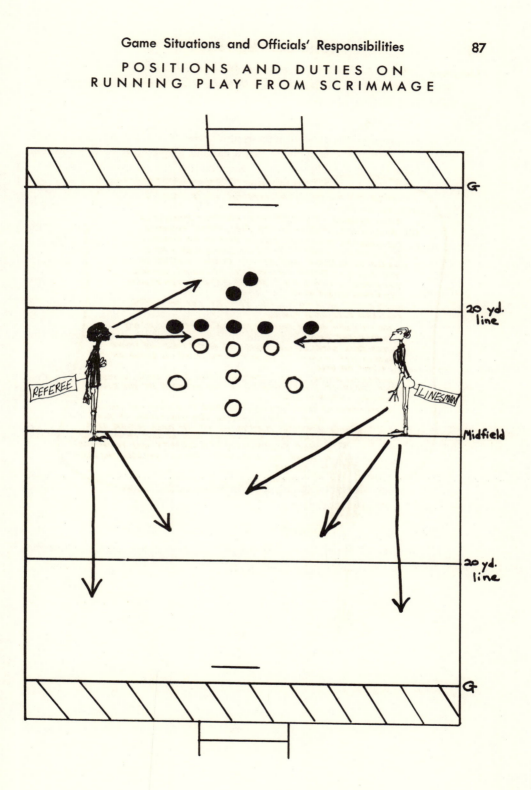

POSITIONS AND DUTIES
ON THE SCRIMMAGE PASS

GENERAL

The initial position for each official is the same as for a running play from scrimmage. As soon as it is apparent that a passing play is developing, however, each official will adjust slightly to fit the situation (see field diagram).

PRIOR TO THE SCRIMMAGE PASS

Referee

The referee should be alert to the following situations prior to the scrimmage pass:

1. Observe all backs behind the line of scrimmage to be certain that they are legal.
2. Observe possible contact with the passer.

Linesman

The linesman should be alert to the following situations prior to the scrimmage pass:

1. Be alert for illegal use of hands and other fouls on the line of scrimmage.
2. If it becomes apparent that a passing play is developing, drift downfield to cover.

AT AND AFTER THE SCRIMMAGE PASS

Specific duties and activities after the scrimmage pass are indicated below.

Referee

If a passing situation should develop from a scrimmage play, the referee should have a few reminders tucked up his sleeve.

Linesman

If a passing situation should develop from a scrimmage play, the linesman must remember specific duties to perform.

REFEREE:

- **OBSERVE THE OFFENSIVE BLOCKING TACTICS CLOSELY**
- OBSERVE POSSIBLE CONTACT WITH THE PASSER
- WATCH THE PASS INSTEAD OF THE FLIGHT OF THE BALL
- BE ALERT TO OBSERVE ANY ILLEGAL PASS AND TO DETERMINE WHETHER THE PASSER IS BEHIND THE LINE OF SCRIMMAGE WHEN HE PASSES THE BALL
- COVER A FUMBLE.
- ON A COMPLETED PASS + AFTER HAVING RECEIVED THE PROPER SIGNAL FROM THE REFEREE, MOVE THE DOWN MARKER TO A POINT PERPENDICULAR TO THE FORWARD MOST POINT OF THE BALL.

REFEREE

- COVER ALL PASSES IN THE SECONDARY. BOTH LONG + SHORT
- WATCH FOR INTERFERENCE BY EITHER TEAM, + BE READY TO RULE ON A POSSIBLE FUMBLE, OR ILLEGAL PASS AFTER.
- BE READY TO CHANGE YOUR MOVEMENT IF THE PROSPECTIVE PASSER DECIDES TO RUN.
- IF THE PASS IS INCOMPLETE, SOUND WHISTLE, STOP CLOCK, + GIVE INCOMPLETE PASS SIGNAL.
- ON AN INCOMPLETE PASS, PROVIDED A PENALTY HAS NOT OCCURRED, RELAY THE BALL TO THE LINESMAN AT THE PREVIOUS LINE OF SCRIMMAGE.
- COVER A FUMBLE OR AN ILLEGAL FORWARD PASS, + THE SPOT OF ANY SUBSEQUENT FOUL.
- SIGNAL LINESMAN TO MOVE DOWN MARKER AFTER A COMPLETE FORWARD PASS, PROVIDED A PENALTY WAS NOT DETECTED OR AFTER THE APPROPRIATE PENALTY YARDAGE HAS BEEN ASSESSED.

POSITIONS AND DUTIES ON
PASSING PLAY FROM SCRIMMAGE

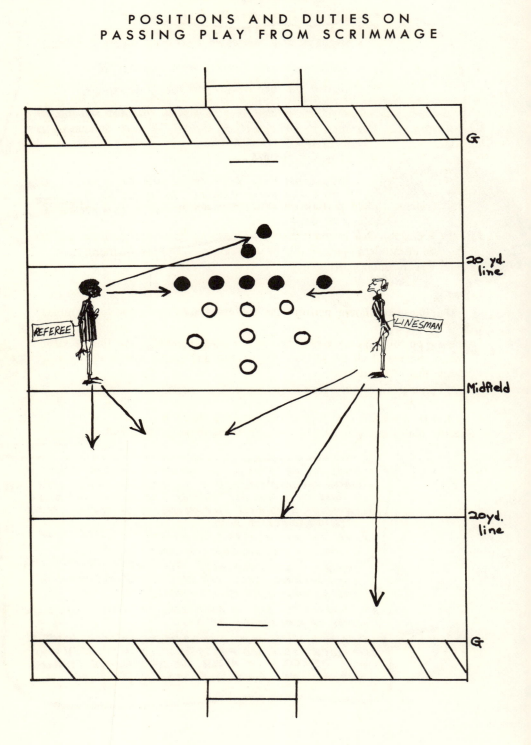

POSITIONS AND DUTIES
ON A SCRIMMAGE KICK

GENERAL

When a scrimmage kick is to be made, the kicking team must announce its desire to kick directly to the referee before the ball is declared ready for play. After such an announcement, the referee must inform the linesman and the defensive team. The kick must be attempted after the kicking team announces its intention.

PRIOR TO A SCRIMMAGE KICK

Referee

The referee should perform the following activities prior to a scrimmage kick:
1. Take a position that is wider than the scrimmage formation position, and on the side of the field opposite that of the linesman (see field diagram).
2. Hold your position until the ball is kicked.

Linesman

The linesman should perform the following activities prior to scrimmage kick:
1. Take a position approximately five to ten yards parallel to the line of scrimmage, outside of all the players in formation and on the side of the field opposite that of the referee.
2. Hold your position until the ball is kicked.

AT AND AFTER THE SCRIMMAGE KICK

Specific duties and activities at and after the scrimmage kick follow.

Referee

As soon as the scrimmage kick has been announced, the referee should begin to contemplate the following:

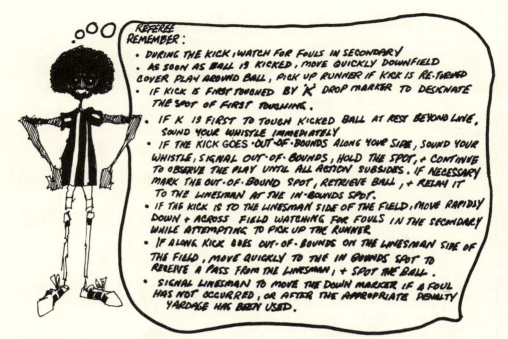

REFEREE
REMEMBER:
• DURING THE KICK, WATCH FOR FOULS IN SECONDARY
• AS SOON AS BALL IS KICKED, MOVE QUICKLY DOWNFIELD COVER PLAY AROUND BALL, PICK UP RUNNER IF KICK IS RE-TURNED
• IF KICK IS FIRST TOUCHED BY 'K' DROP MARKER TO DESIGNATE THE SPOT OF FIRST TOUCHING.
• IF K IS FIRST TO TOUCH KICKED BALL AT REST BEYOND LINE, SOUND YOUR WHISTLE IMMEDIATELY
• IF THE KICK GOES OUT-OF-BOUNDS ALONG YOUR SIDE, SOUND YOUR WHISTLE, SIGNAL OUT-OF-BOUNDS, HOLD THE SPOT, + CONTINUE TO OBSERVE THE PLAY UNTIL ALL ACTION SUBSIDES. IF NECESSARY MARK THE OUT-OF-BOUND SPOT, RETRIEVE BALL, + RELAY IT TO THE LINESMAN AT THE IN-BOUNDS SPOT.
• IF THE KICK IS TO THE LINESMAN SIDE OF THE FIELD, MOVE RAPIDLY DOWN + ACROSS FIELD WATCHING FOR FOULS IN THE SECONDARY WHILE ATTEMPTING TO PICK UP THE RUNNER
• IF A LONG KICK GOES OUT-OF-BOUNDS ON THE LINESMAN SIDE OF THE FIELD, MOVE QUICKLY TO THE IN BOUNDS SPOT TO RECEIVE A PASS FROM THE LINESMAN, + SPOT THE BALL.
• SIGNAL LINESMAN TO MOVE THE DOWN MARKER IF A FOUL HAS NOT OCCURRED, OR AFTER THE APPROPRIATE PENALTY YARDAGE HAS BEEN USED.

Linesman

While waiting for the scrimmage kick to take place, the linesman should be thinking about the following:

LINESMAN SHOULD:
• WATCH FOR FOULS BEHIND THE LINE, ESPECIALLY NEAR KICKER
• UNLESS THE KICK IS TO YOUR SIDE, DELAY + COVER CLIPPING + OTHER FOULS IN THE SECONDARY
• COVER ALL KICKS TO YOUR SIDE OF THE FIELD - AS SOON AS THE BALL IS KICKED, MOVE QUICKLY DOWN FIELD, COVER PLAY AROUND BALL, + PICK UP RUNNER IF KICK IS RETURNED.
• ASSIST THE REFEREE AT THE IN BOUNDS SPOT ON A KICK WHICH GOES OUT-OF-BOUNDS ON HIS SIDE OF THE FIELD.
• COVER OUT-OF-BOUNDS KICK ON YOUR SIDE OF THE FIELD. SOUND WHISTLE, SIGNAL OUT-OF-BOUNDS, HOLD THE SPOT, + CONTINUE TO OBSERVE THE PLAY UNTIL ALL ACTION SUBSIDES. IF NECESSARY, MARK THE OUT-OF-BOUNDS SPOT, RETRIEVE THE BALL, + RELAY IT TO THE REFEREE AT THE CORRESPONDING IN BOUNDS SPOT
• WHEN THE BALL BECOMES DEAD, SOUND YOUR WHISTLE PROMPTLY, + SIGNAL TIME OUT.
• WATCH THE REFEREE FOR A SIGNAL TO MOVE THE DOWN MARKER, BEING CERTAIN THAT NO FOUL HAS OCCURRED

POSITION AND DUTIES DURING
A KICK FROM SCRIMMAGE

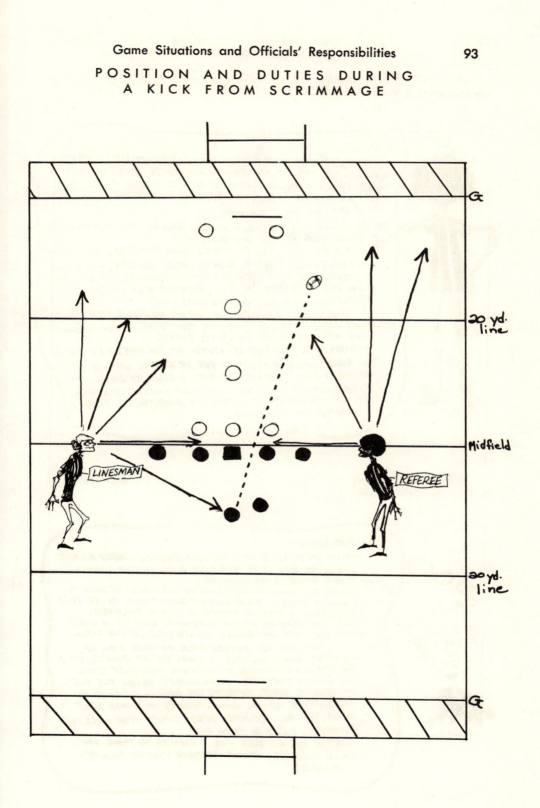

POSITIONS AND DUTIES FOR TRY-FOR-POINT AND FIELD GOAL

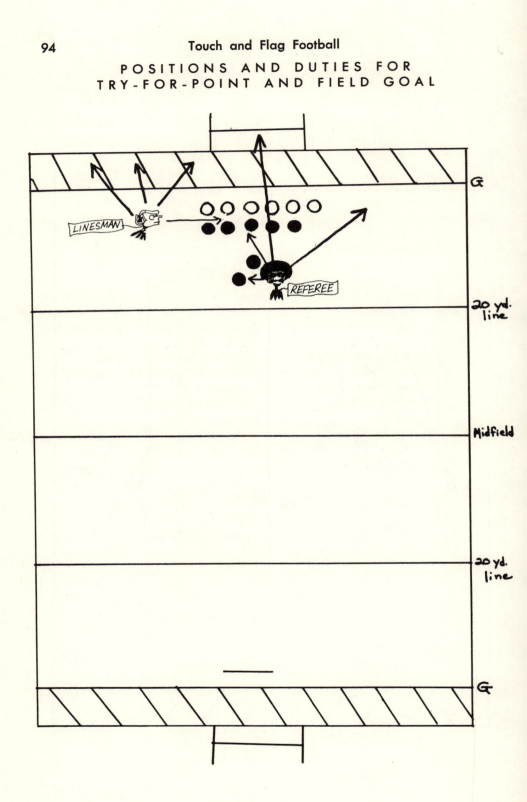

GENERAL

Assume the position indicated by the field diagram. Be alert for pass or run. When the try ends, the referee sounds the whistle and signals score or no score.

AT AND AFTER TRY-FOR-POINT

Specific duties and activities at and after try-for-point are indicated below.

Referee

1. The referee must be behind the kicker to cover acts in his vicinity and to judge whether the kick goes through the goal.
2. When a run develops, check on illegal use of hands and other fouls near the line of scrimmage.
3. On a pass, note whether a pass goes beyond the line of scrimmage.

Linesman

1. The linesman must position himself about five to ten yards outside the defensive end. He should be on the side of the field opposite that of the referee.
2. The linesman must watch for roughness against the kicker or the placekick holder.
3. If a running play develops, watch for fouls in the line of scrimmage.
4. Make sure the ball in possession of a runner touches or crosses the goal line before giving the signal for the touchdown.
5. Be ready to move quickly downfield on a passing situation.

POSITIONS AND DUTIES FOR
GOAL-LINE PLAYS

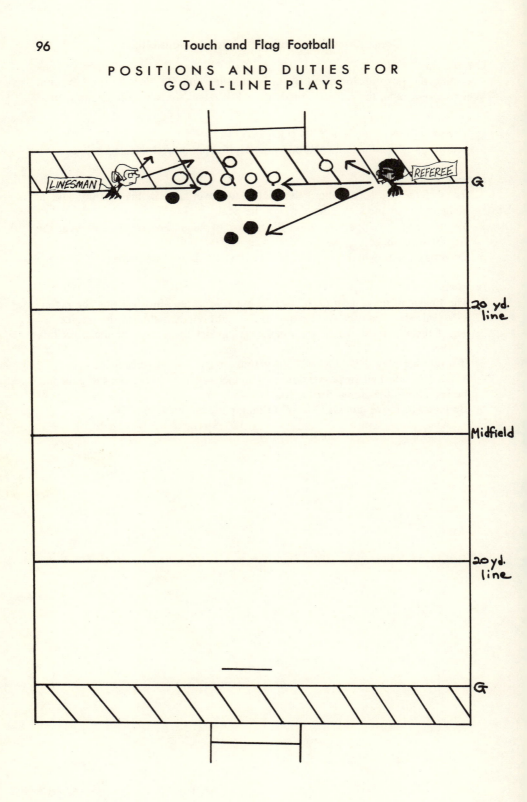

GENERAL

Both the referee and the linesman must take over specific assignments for accurate and instant rulings. Smooth teamwork is imperative. Assume the positions shown in the field diagram.

AT AND AFTER GOAL-LINE PLAY

Referee

The referee should remember the following:
1. Take a normal scrimmage position.
2. Concentrate on the player action on the line, and be alert for a forward pass play.
3. Avoid making a signal if there is any doubt about a touchdown.
4. If you see the ball in possession of a runner touch or cross the goal-line plane, instantly give the touchdown signal.

Linesman

The linesman should remember the following:
1. Observe action on the line.
2. Be ready to drift quickly into the end zone if a forward pass has been thrown.
3. Be alert to detect the farthest point to which the ball is advanced.
4. If you see the ball in possession of a runner touch or cross the goal-line plane, instantly give the touchdown signal.

DECLARING THE BALL READY FOR PLAY

Referee

 After the ball is spotted and the linesman is in position, the referee should move away and give the ready-for-play signal. This is usually done on the first step away from the ball, and the referee should use the whistle to attract attention.

PROCEDURE WHEN TIME-OUT IS DECLARED

GENERAL

 The term *time-out* includes all times when the clock is not running. The time-out signal is given and repeated by the other official. Make a written record if the time-out is charged to a team.

AT AND AFTER TIME-OUT IS SIGNALED

Referee
1. Use your whistle and clearly signal time-out.
2. Get the team captain's approval.
3. Check the number of time-outs charged against the team.

4. Inform each team of the down, distance to gain, and time remaining in the period.
5. Take position over the ball.
6. Keep time with your own watch.
7. Notify the team at sixty seconds.
8. Move to the ball, announce down and distance, and get a ready signal from both captains.
9. Give the ready-for-play signal, sound your whistle, and signal the linesman to start the twenty-five-second count.

Linesman
Maintain a position near the team huddle of the offensive unit.

ADMINISTERING PENALTIES

GENERAL

The duties of administering penalties for the three-man crew are the same as for the two-man crew with the exception of the linesman taking on the additional duties of the umpire. The following are the additional duties of the linesman in a two-man crew:

1. During the administration of all penalties, the linesman shall receive the ball and take it to the spot from which the referee will measure or mark off the penalty.
2. After the referee has measured the penalty and given the appropriate signal, toss the ball to him.
3. Double check the enforcement of the penalty and be certain of the number of the down.
4. Upon receiving the proper signal from the referee, move the down marker to a point perpendicular to the forwardmost point of the ball.

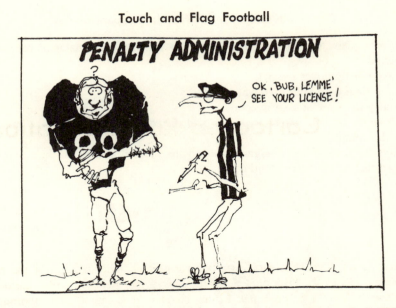

PROCEDURE AT THE END OF THE GAME

GENERAL

The referee and linesman both have specific duties to perform at the end of the game. Basically they are the same as those required of a three-man crew.

The following are the specific duties of the officials at the end of the game:

1. Provide for care of the equipment.
2. The referee should take charge of the game ball at the end of each half and return it to the proper place when the game is over.
3. Do not discuss the game on the field.
4. If there has been any flagrant irregularity, report it as soon as possible to the proper authorities.

5

Cartooned Rule Illustrations

The first prerequisite of a good official is a perfect understanding of the rules and their application. With this in mind, nearly one hundred clear, cartooned rule illustrations will be presented in this chapter. It is important to thoroughly understand the *Official National Touch and Flag Football Rules* in order to become a successful touch and flag football official. To aid the prospective official in interpreting and remembering the rules, all actual playing situations and the captions will explain the rules involved. It is impossible for all the cartooned illustrations and statements to give the complete answer, so it will be necessary to check the *Official National Touch and Flag Football Rules* for technicalities.

TIMING PRINCIPLES AND SUBSTITUTES

The clock running time for touch and flag football games is forty-eight minutes, divided into four periods of twelve minutes duration. An intermission of ten minutes occurs between the second and third periods, and a one-minute rest between the first and second, and third and fourth periods. Any time during the contest, the remaining playing time may be shortened by mutual agreement of the opposing captains and the referee.

The clock starts following a free kick when the ball is legally touched. On a scrimmage down, the game clock is started on the snap or by the referee on a prior signal.

There are several occasions when the clock shall be stopped:
1. On authorized charged time-outs.
2. The ball goes out of bounds.
3. After a valid fair catch as the result of a kick.
4. The ball becomes dead due to a foul or becomes dead behind the goal line.
5. Incomplete pass.
6. The period ends.
7. An attempt of a team to conserve time.
8. An official's time-out.

The referee will start the game clock by a ready-for-play signal if the clock has been stopped due to the following reasons:

1. To complete a penalty.
2. To award a first down.
3. A change of possession with both teams ready for play.
4. At the referee's discretion.
5. By a violation of the substitutes rule, illegal delay, or an excess time-out.

If a free time-out took place in conjunction with the above, or any other incident that would have caused the clock not to start until the ball is put in play, it shall be started when the ball is put in play.

The game clock starts when the ball is put in play with a snap or when a free kick is legally touched if the clock was stopped for the following reasons:

1. A live ball going out of bounds.
2. An incomplete forward pass.
3. A touchback.
4. A legal team time-out.

Two free time-outs during each half without penalty are permitted each team. Consecutive free time-outs will not be permitted the same team.

There are only three violations where substitution is concerned:

1. When a substitute enters during a down.
2. When a player who has been replaced is not off the field before the ball becomes alive.
3. When a substitute is not in uniform ready for play with flags in position.

TIMING PERIODS

Following a kickoff, the game clock shall be started when the ball is legally touched.

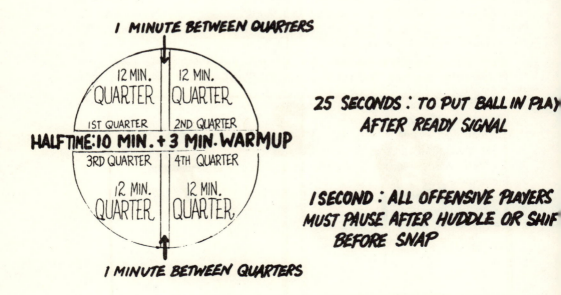

1 MINUTE BETWEEN QUARTERS

12 MIN. QUARTER — 1ST QUARTER

12 MIN. QUARTER — 2ND QUARTER

HALFTIME: 10 MIN. + 3 MIN. WARMUP

3RD QUARTER — 12 MIN. QUARTER

4TH QUARTER — 12 MIN. QUARTER

1 MINUTE BETWEEN QUARTERS

25 SECONDS: TO PUT BALL IN PLAY AFTER READY SIGNAL

1 SECOND: ALL OFFENSIVE PLAYERS MUST PAUSE AFTER HUDDLE OR SHIFT BEFORE SNAP

The referee indicates time-out when a forward pass is incomplete.

Each team is entitled to two free time-outs during each half of the game. Consecutive time-outs shall not be allowed the same team.

Each team is entitled to one-and-one-half minutes during each time-out.

Consuming more than twenty-five seconds in putting the ball in play after it is ready for play is an illegal delay of the game. Penalty: five yards.

When two legal time-outs have been charged to a team in the same half, the referee shall notify the field captain and coach.

The referee does not signal and the game clock starts when the ball is put in play, if it was stopped for the following reasons:

1. Team time-out.
2. Touchback.
3. Incomplete forward pass.
4. Live ball going out of bounds.

The referee shall signal and the game clock starts when the ball is ready for play, if it was stopped for the following reasons:

1. By a violation of the substitution rule, an excess time-out, or an illegal delay.
2. To complete a penalty.
3. To award a first down.
4. After both teams are ready following a change of possession.
5. At the referee's discretion.

The game clock shall be stopped and time is out when each period ends and whenever time-out is declared by the referee. Examples: Touchdown, touchback, field goal, safety, penalty, free time-out, out-of-bounds, or referee's discretion.

The referee may order the game clock started or stopped whenever, in his opinion, either team is trying to conserve or consume playing time by tactics obviously unfair. Penalty: five yards, delay of game.

If the clock was started when it should not have been, the referee will put the time on the clock in order to permit the receivers to put the ball in play.

There is a four-minute warning before each half ends. The referee shall inform each field captain and coach of the playing time remaining in that half.

Play should be resumed when both teams are ready even though the full one-and-one-half minutes is not used during a time-out.

Each substitute shall be in uniform ready for play with flags in position. Penalty: five yards, illegal delay.

When a player who has been replaced is not off the field before the ball becomes alive, it is a foul for illegal substitution. If the penalty is accepted, measure five yards from the spot of the snap.

SCORING

It is a touchdown whenever a live ball in possession of a runner penetrates the plane of the opponent's goal line or touches the goal line. A touchdown could result if the ball in possession of a runner breaks the plane of the goal line without the player entering the end zone. No score will be declared if the player in possession is in the end zone but the ball does not penetrate the plane of the goal line. When a player gets possession of a live ball in his opponent's end zone, it is declared a touchdown.

A field goal is a place kick or a drop kick from scrimmage in flight, other than a try-for-point or a kickoff, whenever the ball passes over the crossbar and over an upright or between the uprights of the receiving team's goal line.

After a touchdown, the scoring team is entitled to a try-for-point from the opponent's three-yard line. There will be one scrimmage play (two points) or a kick (one point). The point shall be awarded if the try results in what would have been a touchdown, or a field goal or safety under rules governing play at other times.

When a runner carries the ball from the field of play to or across his own goal line and it then becomes dead there in his team's possession, it is a safety. It is a safety when a player forces the ball to or across his own goal and it becomes dead there with neither team in possession. This force may come from his kick, pass, snap, muff, or bat, but if a legal forward pass becomes incomplete in the end zone, then this does not apply.

A safety scores two points and the team against whom it is scored must put the ball in play from its own twenty-yard line by a free kick, which may be a dropkick or a placekick.

A safety will result when an accepted penalty for any foul or an illegal forward pass leaves the ball on or behind the offending team's goal line. For example, if an offensive player blocks illegally from within his end zone, it results in two points for his opponent if the penalty is accepted.

When any kick except a successful field goal attempt touches anything while the ball is on or behind the receiving team's goal line, it is a touchback. For a touchback, no points are scored. It is a touchback when a defender intercepts a forward pass in the end zone and the ball becomes dead there.

Following a touchback, the ball shall belong to the defending team at its own twenty-yard line and that team shall put the ball in play by a snap.

The pass is completed in the end zone before the receiver goes out of bounds.

The player controls the ball while in the air, and lands inbounds in the end zone. This results in a touchdown.

A simultaneous catch in the end zone results in a touchdown.

The ball breaks the plane of the goal line without the player entering the end zone.

The player enters the end zone but the ball does not penetrate the plane of the goal line, so this is no score.

When a player causes a live ball to go into his own end zone and it becomes dead there, the result is a safety.

After a safety is scored, the ball shall belong to the defending team at its own twenty-yard line and that team shall put the ball in play by a free kick, which may be a dropkick or a placekick.

A successful attempt when the ball is between the uprights and breaks the plane of the crossbar and is above the crossbar: this is a field goal.

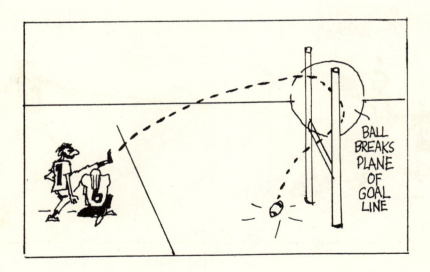

The ball becomes dead when downed in the end zone on the kickoff.

B intercepts and is downed in his end zone. The force came from A's pass. It is a touchback if the ball becomes dead in B's possession in the end zone.

BALL IN PLAY, DEAD BALL, AND OUT-OF-BOUNDS

The kickoff puts a ball in play at the start of each half and resumes play after a field goal or a try-for-point. Whenever a free kick is not specified, the ball will be put in play by a snap. After being put in play, the ball remains alive until the down ends.

Situations in which the ball becomes dead and the down is ended are:

1. When the runner goes out of bounds or when the ball touches the goal line of the ball-carrier's opponents.
2. When any part of the ball-carrier's person other than his hand or foot touches the ground.
3. When a ball carrier has a flag removed legally by a defensive player or if a ball carrier accidentally drops his flag.
4. When a ball carrier is legally touched between the shoulders and knees, including the hand and arm.
5. When a touchdown, field goal, touchback, safety, or successful try-for-point is made.
6. When a member of the kicking team catches or recovers any free kick or a scrimmage kick that is beyond the neutral zone; also, when a free kick or an untouched scrimmage kick comes to rest on the ground and no player attempts to secure it.
7. When a forward pass is incomplete or is caught simultaneously by opposing players.
8. When a fumble or a backward pass touches the ground and when the ball, snapped from scrimmage, touches the ground before or after getting to the intended receiver.

A player is declared out of bounds when any part of his person touches anything other than another player or a game official who is on or outside a boundary line. A ball carrier is declared out of bounds when either the ball or any part of the runner touches the ground or anything else, except a game official or a player who is on or outside a boundary line.

A team in possession of the ball is awarded a series of four consecutive downs to advance to the next zone by scrimmage. A new series is awarded if the ball belongs to the offensive team on or beyond the zone to gain. It is also a new series and the ball will belong to the defensive team at the end of any down provided the defensive team gained possession during that down or at the end of any fourth down, if the offensive team was in possession behind the zone to gain.

The ball is declared dead when the ball carrier accidentally drops his flag.

The ball is dead when the ball carrier hits the ground and not to where he slides.

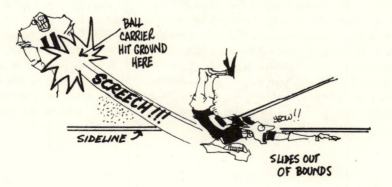

When a contest by defenders causes an eligible receiver, who is airborne, to first contact the ground out of bounds, the pass is ruled complete if the receiver would have landed inbounds had there been no contact. This is a complete pass.

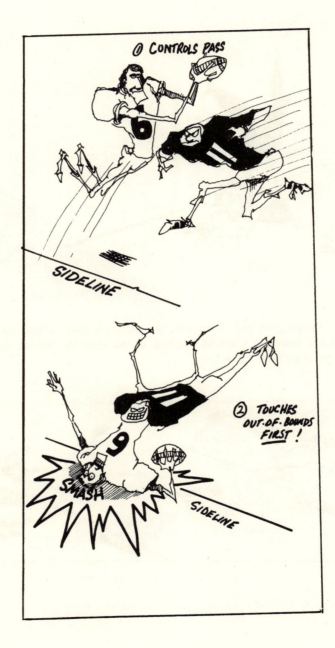

When the ball, in possession of a runner, goes out of bounds, the inbounds spot is the yard line through the foremost part of the ball when the runner crosses the plane of the sideline.

When a runner goes out of bounds, the inbounds spot is fixed by the yard line through the foremost point of the ball at the time the runner crossed the sideline. There is no new series here.

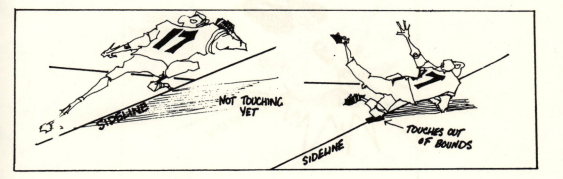

The ball is dead when the ball-carrier's knee touches the ground.

A dead ball may become alive only by a snap or free kick. After being put in play, the ball remains alive until the down is ended.

A ball snapped from scrimmage that hits the ground before or after getting to the intended receiver is dead at the spot at which it hit the ground.

The ball is declared dead when a ball carrier is legally touched between the shoulders and knees, including the hand and arm.

The ball is declared dead when the ball-carrier's flag is removed by a defensive player.

A runner may carry the ball over the out-of-bounds area and it will remain in play, provided neither the ball nor the runner touches out of bounds. Here the advance by #69 is legal.

"69" MAKES IT SAFELY INBOUNDS AGAIN, SINCE NEITHER BALL OR FEET *TOUCHED* OUT OF BOUNDS.....

SIDELINE

SIDELINE

KICKS AND FAIR CATCH

If it is not moved by a penalty, the kicking team's free kick line for a kick-off is the twenty-yard line on fields one hundred yards long. The kickoff may be put in play by a placekick or a dropkick from a spot on or behind the kicking team's restraining line and between the inbounds lines. Following a safety, a dropkick or placekick may be used. The game clock is not started until the kick is legally touched.

All players of the kicking team must be inbounds and all players, except the holder and kicker of a placekick, must be behind their restraining line when the ball is legally kicked. At least three players of the receiving team in the seven-man game must be within five yards of their restraining line until the ball is kicked.

During a kickoff, no player of the kicking team shall touch the ball before it reaches the receiver's restraining line. No member of the kicking team may interfere with the receiving team's opportunity to catch the ball. If the kickoff is caught or recovered by a member of the receiving team, the ball continues in play; but if a member of the kicking team catches or recovers the kickoff, the ball becomes dead.

During any down, the offensive team may placekick, dropkick, or punt from behind its scrimmage line before possession has changed. Such a kick is a scrimmage kick. When a scrimmage kick is to be made, the kicking team must announce it to the referee before the ball is declared ready for play. A member of the kicking team may not touch a scrimmage kick that goes beyond the neutral zone before it touches an opponent. If this occurs, the receiving team has the option of taking the ball at the spot of the touching when the ball becomes dead. If a player of either team touches a scrimmage kick that then touches the ground, it is dead at the spot of touching the ground. This ball belongs to the receiving team at that spot or at the spot of first touching by the kicking team.

Any member of the receiving team may signal for a fair catch of any kick. A player of a team or his teammate who has signaled for a fair catch may not advance the ball more than two steps in any direction. A fair catch signaled by a player whose teammate then makes the catch is not considered a fair catch and the ball becomes dead.

The kicking team's restraining line on kickoffs shall be its twenty-yard line on fields one hundred yards long unless relocated by penalty.

At least three players of the receiving team in seven-man formation must be within five yards of their restraining line until the ball is kicked.

The kicking team must announce to the referee before the ball is declared ready for play when a scrimmage kick is to be made.

A scrimmage kick that touches a player of either team and then touches the ground is dead at the spot of touching the ground and belongs to the receiving team at that spot or at the spot of first touching by the kicking team.

A ball that strikes the ground before or after reaching the kicker on a scrimmage kick is dead at the spot at which it struck the ground and it is a loss of down.

This blocked punt goes out of bounds behind the line of scrimmage. The ball will belong to the receiving team at the inbounds spot, regardless of the down and yardage when the scrimmage kick was made.

If a free kick goes out of bounds untouched between the restraining lines, the receiving team will put the ball in play on the inbounds spot on the line opposite the out-of-bounds spot.

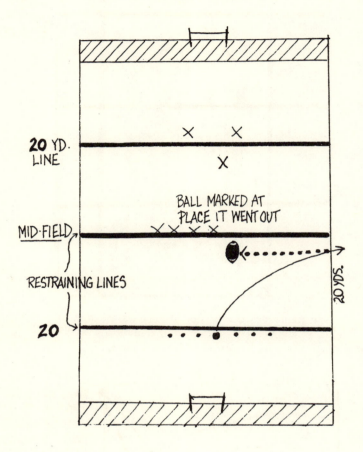

If a free kick that is touched by either team goes out of bounds before touching the ground after being touched between the goal lines, the ball belongs to the receiving team at the inbounds spot on the line opposite the out-of-bounds spot.

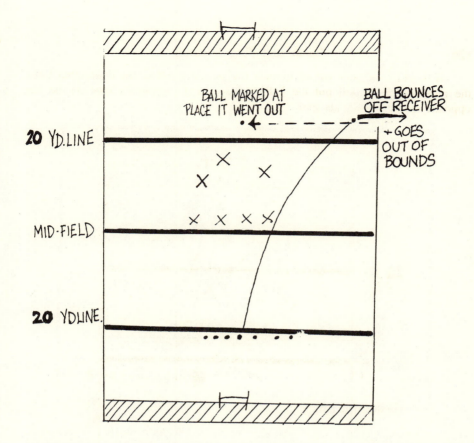

If a free kick goes out of bounds behind the goal line, it is a touchback and the ball belongs to the team defending that goal line at the twenty-yard line.

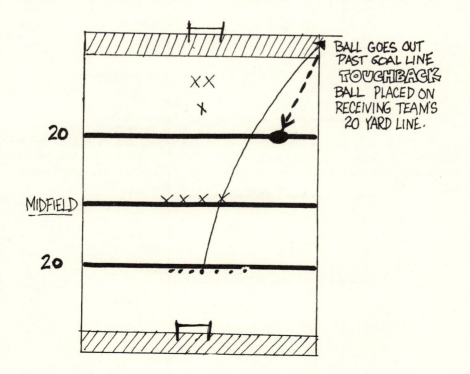

A free kick touched by a player of the receiving team that then touches the ground is dead at the spot at which it touches the ground and belongs to the receiving team.

If a free kick goes out of bounds untouched beyond the receiving team's restraining line but between the goal lines, the ball is put in play at the receiving team's restraining line.

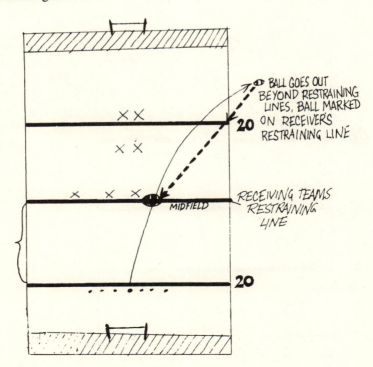

On a kick that passes through the plane of the sideline while in the air, but falls inside the playing field, it is not out of bounds.

If a player of the kicking team who is beyond the neutral zone catches or recovers a scrimmage kick, the ball becomes dead and belongs to the receiving team.

Illustration 1 is an example of a valid fair-catch signal. Illustrations 2, 3, and 4 are examples of invalid fair-catch signals and are classed as unsportsmanlike.

CONDUCT OF PLAYERS
AND OTHERS SUBJECT TO THE RULES

Since flag and touch football are both vigorous personal contact games, it is necessary to protect the players through strict regulations.

If in the judgment of any game official, the following acts are deliberate or flagrant, the involved players may be suspended: using fists, kneeing or kicking, roughing the kicker or holder of a kick, tackling the ball carrier as in regulation football, or any other deliberate or flagrant act.

Unsportsmanlike conduct by players, substitutes, coaches, or others will not be tolerated. Such acts as abusive or insulting language, using the "hideout" play, the punter delaying the kick after requesting protection, or pulling or removing the flag from an offensive player by a defensive player as the ball is snapped or during the play with the obvious intent of making the offensive player ineligible to become a pass receiver or ball carrier, could result in a penalty of fifteen yards; and if flagrant, the offender shall be disqualified.

Players are further restricted by certain actions or any other act of unnecessary roughness, which will be a personal foul. A personal foul will result in a fifteen-yard penalty, and if flagrant, the offenders may be disqualified. Some examples of such acts are: no player shall block in a manner that would cause his feet, knees, or legs to strike an opponent; no two-on-one blocking exept as indicated by the rules; no high-low blocking; no tripping; no clipping; and no hurdling.

To ensure balance between the offense and defense, definite restrictions are placed upon each. An offensive player is restricted in the use of his hands and arms, while the defensive player may use his hands to push or pull an opponent in order to get at a runner or to ward off a blocker. To strike an opponent with the hand, forearm, or elbow and for either team to lock his hands when contacting an opponent with the hands is always a foul. A player is always prohibited from using his hand and arm for the purpose of punishing or injuring an opponent.

BLOCKING

In all instances, a blocker must be on his feet when blocking. When a teammate of a ball carrier or passer uses a hand or forearm in blocking or to supplement a shoulder block, a hand must be in contact with the blocker's body and the hand and arm kept below the shoulders of the opponent during the entire block.

The blocker's hands may not be locked nor may he swing, throw, or whip his elbow or forearm so that it is moving faster than the blocker's shoulder at the time the elbow, forearm, or shoulder contacts the opponent.

In a crab or body block, it is not required that the hand or arm be in contact with the blocker's body.

Whenever a blocker's arm is in contact with his opponent, the blocker's hand shall be in contact with his body.

Penalty: fifteen yards.

Teammates of a ball carrier or passer may interfere for him by blocking, but there shall be no interlocking interferences. This prohibition includes grasps or encircling one another, to any degree, with the hand or arm.

Penalty: fifteen yards from spot of foul.

The following illustrations are acts that are deliberate or flagrant fouls. The above include: using fists, kicking or kneeing an opponent.

There shall be no hurdling. Hurdling shall be interpreted as an attempt by the runner to jump over a player with both feet or knees of the runner foremost. Penalty: fifteen yards, and flagrant offenders may be disqualified.

It is a personal foul to throw the runner to the ground.
Penalty: fifteen yards, and flagrant offenders may be disqualified.

No player may leave the ground with both feet in an attempt to gain possession of a kicked ball, untouched, that is rolling on the ground.
Penalty: Offended team's ball at spot of foul.

There shall be no high-low blocking.
Penalty: fifteen yards, and if flagrant, offenders may be disqualified.

Two-on-one blocking shall be limited to the area on and behind the neutral zone.
Penalty: fifteen yards.

A defensive player shall not hold, grasp, or obstruct forward progress of a ball carrier when in the act of removing a flag.

Penalty: fifteen yards from spot of foul.

In flag football, the ball carrier shall not deliberately drive or run into a defensive player.

Penalty: fifteen yards; if flagrant, offenders may be disqualified.

Players may use their hands to grasp, push, or pull an opponent in an attempt to get at the ball carrier and may also use their hands for protection in warding off an opponent, or to get at a free ball.

An act of unsportsmanlike conduct occurs when a defensive player pulls or removes a flag from an offensive player as the ball is snapped or during a play with the obvious intent of making the offensive player ineligible to become a pass receiver or ball carrier.

Penalty: fifteen yards, and if flagrant, offender shall be disqualified.

The ball carrier shall not grasp a teammate or be grasped, pulled, or pushed by a teammate.

Penalty: five yards from spot of foul.

The ball carrier shall not protect his flags by blocking with his arms or hands the opportunity of an opponent to pull or remove his flags.

Penalty: fifteen yards from the spot of the foul.

An act of unsportsmanlike conduct occurs when abusive or insulting language is used.

Penalty: fifteen yards, and if flagrant, offenders shall be disqualified.

An act of unsportsmanlike conduct occurs when a team uses a "hide out play" by placing a player or players near the sideline who were not within fifteen yards of the ball at the ready-for-play signal.

Penalty: fifteen yards, and if flagrant, offender shall be disqualified.

It might be considered a deliberate or flagrant act when using a karate chop on the passer.

If in the judgment of any game official the above acts are deliberate or flagrant, the players involved shall be suspended.

It is a personal foul to use locked hands, elbows, or any part of the forearm or hand, except according to rules.

It is a personal foul to tackle the ball carrier as in regulation football.

It is a personal foul to trip or clip an opponent.
Penalty: fifteen yards, and flagrant offenders may be disqualified.

SCRIMMAGE, SNAPPING, HANDLING, AND PASSING

The use of the snap and free kick are the two ways to put the ball in play in touch and flag football.

All offensive players must be within fifteen yards of the ball following the ready-for-play signal and prior to the snap. The offensive team must have at least three players on the offensive line when there are seven players on a team, five men on the offensive line when there are nine players, and seven men on the offensive line when there are eleven players on a team. In order for a player to be considered on the line, he must be within twelve inches of his line facing the opponent's goal line with his shoulders parallel to the line. A player must be at least one yard from the line to be considered off the line. With the exception of the man in the position to receive a hand-to-hand snap, all backfield men must be at least one yard behind the ball.

Several types of illegal actions by both offensive and defensive teams will be illustrated in this section.

No player may hand the ball forward except to a player in certain situations listed below:

1. An offensive player who is behind the line of scrimmage may hand the ball forward to a backfield teammate who is also behind that line.
2. An offensive player who is behind the line of scrimmage may hand the ball forward to a teammate who was on his scrimmage line when the ball was snapped, provided that the teammate left his line position, faced his own end line, and was at least one yard behind his scrimmage line when he received the ball.

At anytime, a ball carrier may hand the ball backward.

Only the team that has put the ball in play from scrimmage may throw a forward pass. A pass may be defined as a ball traveling in flight that is thrown rather than handed. Each pass must be thrown from in or behind the neutral zone, and any number of legal forward passes from behind the line of scrimmage is permitted. During a forward pass, all players of the team are eligible to touch or catch it.

A forward pass is illegal in the following situations, and is penalized by a loss of five yards from the spot of the foul.

1. When a pass is thrown from beyond the defensive line of scrimmage.
2. When more than one forward pass beyond the line of scrimmage is made.
3. When a pass is thrown after a change of team possession.
4. When a pass is intentionally thrown to the ground or out of bounds.

Several types of illegal action of both offensive and defensive teams will be illustrated in this section.

At least three players on the offensive line (seven players) must be on their scrimmage line. To be considered on the line players must be within twelve inches of the line of scrimmage and shoulders must be parallel to and facing the opponents' goal line.

12 INCHES

Any number of forward passes may be thrown during a down provided all are thrown from behind the line of scrimmage and there was no change of team possession.

There is no pass interference if two or more players are making a simultaneous and bona fide attempt to reach, catch, or bat the pass.

A backward pass or fumble that touches the ground is dead at the spot where it touches the ground and belongs to the team last in possession.

Either offensive or defensive man may legally interfere with opponents in the neutral zone or behind the offensive scrimmage line.

To be legal, a forward pass must leave the passer's hand on his side of the defensive team's line of scrimmage. The pass may be thrown from within the original neutral zone.

One offensive player may be in motion but not in motion toward his opponent's goal line.

A forward pass is illegally thrown if intentionally thrown to the ground or out of bounds. Penalty: five yards from spot of foul.

A backward pass or fumble may be caught in flight by any player and advanced.

If a pass is caught simultaneously by opponents, the ball becomes dead and belongs to the passing team at that spot.

It is illegal to "play through" a man in order to get the ball during a forward pass. In this illustration it will be defensive interference.

Officials must consider time periods when determining whether there is pass interference:

1. The defender may use his hands to ward off a potential receiver prior to the time the forward pass is in flight.
2. It is a foul to contact or hinder an opponent's opportunity to move toward the ball, which is in flight.
3. If the forward pass crosses the line of scrimmage, it will be a foul for offensive interference.

Defensive pass interference: here #81 has directed his attention to the receiver, which indicates an intent to hinder the receiver rather than catch or bat the ball. It is therefore interference.

ENFORCEMENT OF PENALTIES

The referee will, at the end of the down, inform both captains whenever a foul is reported. He will inform the offended captain of the results of accepting the play, or the penalty. In the process the referee will indicate the down and distance for each option.

The official shall not permit the ball to become alive when a foul occurs during a dead ball between downs or prior to a free kick or snap. The offended captain will then be presented with the options.

There are several enforcement reminders when a double or multiple foul occurs. Some of these are:

1. If fouls by both teams are reported to the referee before the penalty before any one of them has been completed, it is considered a double foul and the penalties are offsetting. The down is replayed.
2. If two or more fouls by the same team are reported, only one penalty may be measured or the offended captain may decline all penalties.
3. During a down where there was a double foul followed by a dead-ball foul, it will not be considered part of a multiple foul even though it may occur prior to the referee explaining the options to the captain. The dead-ball foul will be administered separately and from the succeeding spot, and the double-foul penalties will offset.

4. The penalties are administered separately and in the order of occurrence if a live-ball foul by one team is followed by a dead-ball foul by the opponent.
5. Dead-ball fouls are administered separately and in the order of their occurrence.
6. When there is a change of team possession and both teams foul during this down, the team last gaining possession may keep the ball provided its foul was not prior to the final change of possession and it declined the penalty for its opponent's foul.

Ordinarily, the enforcement spot is the spot specified in the penalty. However, when no such spot is fixed or when the time of the foul affects the enforcement, then the principles listed below will be helpful:

1. If a foul occurs during a free kick, scrimmage kick, or during a legal forward pass, the basic spot is the previous spot.
2. If a foul occurs during a running play, the basic enforcement spot is the spot where the run ends.

When administering penalties, there are a few principles to keep in mind:

1. The enforcement spot for a foul committed when the ball is dead is the succeeding spot.
2. If a foul occurs simultaneously with a snap or free kick, the penalty will be enforced from the previous spot.
3. For a foul during a running play or loose-ball play, the penalty is from the basic spot unless the foul was by the offense and it occurred behind the basic spot. In that case, it is from the spot of the foul.

It is not a foul if the defensive team member goes into the neutral zone and gets back before the snap.

It is encroachment when contact is made with an opponent even though #40 withdraws before the snap is made. This is a dead ball foul and the official will not permit the ball to be snapped and become alive.

If the offense commits a pass interference foul during a try-for-point and the try is unsuccessful, no point is scored and there is no replay.

Not a double foul. The defensive team may retain possession if the penalty for the offside is declined. The clipping at 3 and 5 will be penalized separately and in the order of occurrence.

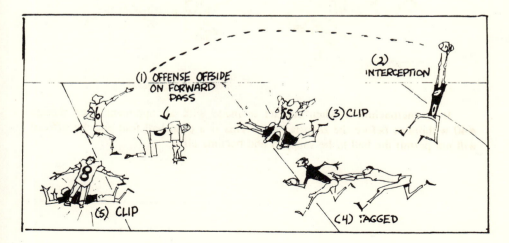

No penalty directly results in a safety, but if a distance penalty is measured from behind the offender's goal line toward his endline, it is a safety. Here the offensive halfback holds behind the goal line. The penalty is measured from the spot toward the endline, hence it is a safety.

1. *False Start:* When a offensive player charges and causes reflex action by the defensive man, the foul is on the man making the initial charge.
2. *Encroachment:* When a defensive player charges and causes reflex action by the offensive man, the foul is on the man making the initial charge.

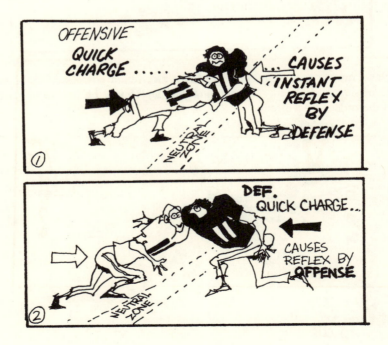

During a try-for-point by running, the offensive is offside. After the tag, a defensive player clips. Because the try-for-point was unsuccessful and the offense fouled, there will be no replay for the try-for-point. The penalty for the dead-ball foul by the defense will be penalized on the ensuing kickoff.

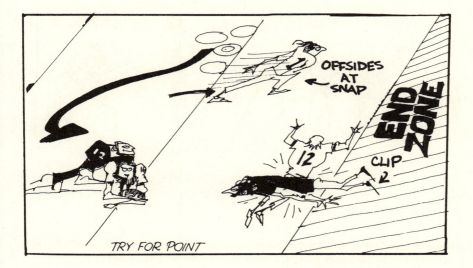

The defensive team will accept the penalty for this foul and the offense will replay the try from the eighteen-yard line.

No foul causes loss of the ball. Here the foul occurred before the ball carrier crossed the goal line. The enforcement spot is where the run ended (the goal line). While there is no touchdown, the offense will again put the ball in play after being penalized to defensive fifteen-yard line.

The live-ball fouls by both teams combine to make a double foul and the down will be replayed. The clip is a dead-ball foul and will be separately administered from the previous spot.

The basic spot is the end of the run, and the penalty for the holding by the defensive player will be measured from that spot.

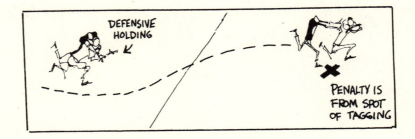

The penalty for a dead-ball foul is measured from the spot at which the ball will next be put in play (succeeding spot).

The defensive team may decline the penalty for the offside and retain possession. The penalty for the clipping will be administered separately.

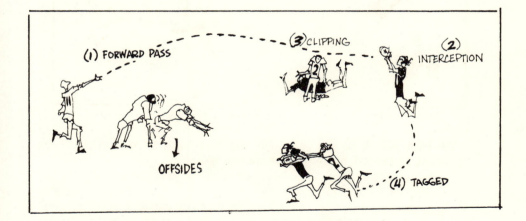

During a kick, legal pass behind the line of scrimmage, if the offense fouls behind the line the penalty is from the spot of the foul.

OFFENSE FOULS
BEHIND LINE
OF SCRIMMAGE

No live ball foul causes the official to sound his whistle immediately. Here the play goes through to completion even though a member of kicking team is held while the punt was in the air. The kicking team will have the option of accepting the penalty and replaying the down or of accepting the results of the play.

This is not a multiple foul because all dead ball fouls are to be penalized. Penalize the holding from the spot of the foul and the clipping from the succeeding spot.

The false start by #8 and the personal foul by #76 will both be penalized because they are dead-ball fouls. The penalties will be measured in the order of occurrence. The offense will be penalized five yards from the spot of the snap. Then the fifteen-yard penalty against defense will be measured.

All fouls but one are penalized from the basic spot, which, during the running play, is where the run ended. The one foul that is not penalized from the basic spot is the one by the offense behind that spot which may have aided the runner in gaining. In this case, the penalty by the offensive lineman will be administered from the spot of the foul.

6
Officials'
Self-Analysis

THE OFFICIALS'
JURISDICTION AND RESPONSIBILITIES

Answer the following self-analysis questions true or false. Answers found on page 168.

1. The official who is covering the ball is primarily responsible for sounding the whistle when the ball becomes dead.
2. All officials should carry their whistles.
3. The first responsibility of any official is the safety of the players.
4. The ball becomes dead if a whistle is sounded inadvertently.
5. The referee in a three-man crew is responsible for inspecting the field during the pregame duties.

6. The umpire in a three-man crew is responsible for securing the down marker during the pregame duties.

7. The visiting captain should be instructed by the referee during the coin-toss ceremony to call heads or tails while the coin is in the air.

8. The referee will indicate the coin-toss winner by placing a hand on his shoulder.

9. The only choice the coin winner has is to decide whether to kick or receive.

10. As soon as the ball is legally kicked, all officials will signal the clock to start.

11. If an official accidentally sounds his whistle during a kick, the ball is dead at the spot of catch.

12. The referee after spotting the ball should announce the number of the down and distance to go.

13. It is a good procedure for the official to note the location of the ball at the time of the foul.

14. All officials should check on the administration of the penalty.

15. The nearest official should signal time-out, hold the spot, and continue to observe play when the ball goes out of bounds.

16. To speed up action between downs, it is advisable for the officials to toss the ball underhanded.

17. On scrimmage runs, it is advisable to continue to observe the play after dropping a marker.

19. All officials should mark which team has first choice for the second half.

20. The referee should face each sideline after walking off a penalty and give the proper signal for the foul.

THREE-MAN CREW
JURISDICTION AND RESPONSIBILITIES

21. It is the duty of the linesman prior to a free kick to count the receiving team players.

22. The primary responsibility of the referee during a free kick is to pick up the runner and follow.

23. The umpire should move to a position back of the offense on the side opposite the linesman for a scrimmage play.

24. The linesman should always position himself on the sideline during a scrimmage play.

25. The referee should watch the passer instead of the flight of the ball.

26. It is the responsibility of the referee to determine if the passer released the ball on his side of the defensive scrimmage line.

27. The umpire should cover short passes down the middle.

28. The linesman on a pass play should drift downfield to cover passes on his sideline.

29. During a goal-line play, the linesman is responsible to see if the ball touched or crossed the goal-line plane.

30. The referee after receiving the full information from the other official(s) should immediately walk off the penalty.
31. After the referee spots the ball, he should step away and announce the down and distance to go.
32. The primary responsibility of the umpire during the administration of all penalties should be to hold the spot from which the penalty will be measured.
33. The umpire is responsible for keeping the game time.
34. After the ball has gone downfield on a free kick, the linesman should move in that direction while watching for clips, illegal use of hands, etc.
35. It is the responsibility of the umpire to pick up the runner if a long scrimmage kick is returned.

TWO-MAN CREW
JURISDICTION AND RESPONSIBILITIES

36. It is the responsibility of the referee prior to a free kick to count the receiving team players.
37. At the free kick, the linesman should move to a position on the sideline even with the kicking team's restraining line.
38. The linesman is responsible for picking up the runner on a free kick.
39. At the free kick, the referee is responsible for offside violations by the kicking team.
40. During a passing play, it is the responsibility of the referee to observe possible contact with the passer.
41. During a scrimmage kick, it is the responsibility of the referee to pick up the runner.
42. During a field goal attempt, the referee should position himself behind the kicker.
43. During the administration of all penalties, the linesman should take the ball to the spot from which the referee will measure or mark off the penalty.
44. At the free kick, the referee should be alert to first touching of the kick by a member of the kicking team before it crosses the receiving team's restraining line.
45. The referee should keep the game time.
46. Each play should be properly boxed in at all times.
47. Prior to the snap, the referee should position himself straddling the neutral zone five to ten yards from the nearest player.
48. It is the responsibility of the linesman to check the twenty-five-second count.
49. Due to the fact that only two officials are working the game, the referee should follow the runner very closely on runs to the linesman side.
50. If a wide run develops to the linesman side and he is unable to retreat fast enough, he may turn his back to the play and run downfield to cover the play.

TIMING PRINCIPLES

51. The clock has been stopped to award a first down and there has been no charged time-out during that dead-ball period. Is the official correct in starting the clock by a ready-for-play signal?

52. During a free kick, the ball hits the ground and is then picked up by the receiver. Is the official correct in starting the clock when the ball was legally kicked?

53. The clock has been stopped for an incomplete forward pass and there has been no charged time-out during that dead-ball period. Is the official correct in starting the clock by a ready-for-play signal?

54. There are five seconds left in the second period and Team A runs a play in which a personal foul was committed by Team B. Time runs out during the play. Is the official correct in indicating end of the period?

55. After a Team A time-out, the referee has declared the ball ready-for-play and then he notices that a member of Team A is wearing some illegal equipment. The referee calls time-out and charges the time-out to Team A. Is the official correct in indicating this action?

56. With five seconds left in the fourth period, the quarterback throws a legal forward pass to his receiver who runs the ball to the ten-yard line. Before he is tagged, the game time runs out. During the play an offensive player committed a clip. Is the official correct in indicating the period is to be extended?

57. After the twenty-five-second count, the official was certain that the offense was stalling. Is the official correct in indicating illegal delay of game penalty and starting the clock on the ready-for-play signal?

58. The clock has been stopped because of change of possession and there has been no charged time-out during that dead-ball period. Is the official correct in starting the clock with the snap of the ball?

59. It is the beginning of the third period and getting dark. By mutual agreement the two team captains and the referee agree to shorten the remaining period. Is the official correct in this action?

60. Team A scores a touchdown. At the snap for the try-for-point, the umpire starts the clock. Is the umpire correct in starting the clock for the try-for-point?

BALL IN PLAY, DEAD BALL, OUT-OF-BOUNDS

61. While a receiver attempts to gain possession of a kick, he touches the ball while one of his feet is on the sideline. Is the official correct in indicating inbounds?

62. During a running play from scrimmage, the ball carrier accidentally drops his flag and goes for a touchdown. Is the official correct in indicating a touchdown?

63. During a pass play, the right offensive end catches the pass and is running when he slips and falls to the ground. As his knee hits the ground, the ball pops up into the air, where it is caught by a defensive back. He then advances for a touchdown. Is the official correct in indicating a touchdown?

64. During a free kick, a receiver signals a legal fair catch on his fifteen-yard line. The kick is over his head and the ball rolls to the five-yard line with both teams refusing to touch it. Is the official correct in indicating dead ball and receiving team's ball at the five-yard line?

65. During a scrimmage kick, the ball strikes the ground and bounces into the air near the sideline. The receiver controls the ball in the air and lands out of bounds. He attempts to advance the ball. Is the official correct in indicating dead ball, the kick out of bounds, and the receiving teams will put the ball in play at inbounds spot?

66. During a running play, the right offensive halfback, Al, fumbles the ball. It strikes the ground and it is recovered by a defensive back, B1. He then advances the ball to the five-yard line. Is the official correct in indicating B's ball, first down, on the five-yard line?

67 .During a free kick, K1 first touches the ball beyond the receiving team's restraining line. He then advances the ball to the twenty-five-yard line. Is the official correct in indicating K's ball first down on the twenty-five-yard line?

68. During a running play, the ball carrier, Al, is tagged on the arm at midfield. The official lets the play continue with Al advancing to the twenty-two-yard line. Is the official correct in indicating A's ball on twenty-two-yard line?

69. During a scrimmage play, the quarterback fakes to the right halfback, Al. He keeps the ball and rolls out and passes to his left end for a touchdown. The official had inadvertently sounded his whistle when the right halfback, Al, got tagged. He thought the right halfback was carrying the ball. Is the official correct in indicating a dead ball immediately and the down will be replayed?

70. During a scrimmage kick, while R1 was waiting to receive the kick, the official accidentally sounded his whistle. However R1 received the ball and advanced to midfield. Is the official correct in indicating R's ball first down at midfield?

KICKS AND FAIR CATCH

71. During a free kick, a receiver indicates a legal fair catch signal and catches the ball. He then advances the ball forward for two steps and decides to stop. Is the official correct in indicating illegal delay of game, loss of five yards?

72. During a scrimmage kick, a member of the kicking team, K1, is beyond the neutral zone and first touches the ball. He then advances the ball to midfield. Is the official correct in indicating K's ball first down, midfield?

73. During a free kick, the ball goes out of bounds untouched beyond the receiving team's restraining line but between the goal lines. Is the official correct in indicating the ball will be put in play at the inbounds spot on the line opposite the out of bounds?

74. During a free kick, the ball strikes a receiving team player, R1, who is in his end zone. The ball goes out of bounds at the two-yard line. Is the official correct in indicating a touchback?

75. During a free kick, the ball goes beyond the restraining line of the receiving team. It is first touched by a member of the kicking team, K1. He then advances the ball and fumbles, with K2 recovering. Is the official correct in indicating K's ball at spot of fumble?

76. During a free kick, a receiving team player in an attempt to catch the kick is touched before the ball arrives by a kicking team player. However he catches the ball in flight and is tagged. Is the official correct in indicating illegal interference, R's ball, first down, loss of fifteen yards beyond the spot of foul?

77. During a free kick, a receiving team player in an attempt to catch the kick is touched before the ball arrives by a member of the kicking team. The receiver fumbles the ball. Is the official correct in indicating R's ball first down at spot of fumble?

78. During a free kick, the ball goes out of bounds untouched between the restraining lines. Is the official correct in indicating that the ball will be put in play at the receiving team's restraining line?

79. During a free kick, a member of the kicking team touches the ball before it reaches the opponent's restraining line. Is the official correct in indicating the receiving team's ball where first touched by the kicking team player?

80. During a scrimmage kick, the ball fails to cross the neutral zone. The ball is recovered by a member of the kicking team and advanced. Is the official correct in indicating legal play?

SCORING

81. During a pass play, a defensive back, B1, interferes with the right offensive end, A1, while the ball is in the air and they are both in the end zone. Is the official correct in indicating a touchdown?

82. During a pass play, a defensive back, B1, intercepts a forward pass in his end zone. As he attempts to run out he is tagged by an opponent while still in the end zone. Is the official correct in indicating a safety?

83. During a pass play, a defensive back, B1, intercepts a pass on his five-yard line. He runs backward into his own end zone. He then fumbles the ball and it bounces in the end zone and goes out of bounds. Is the official correct in indicating a touchdown?

84. After a safety is scored, is the official correct in giving possession to the defending team at its own twenty-yard line and that team shall put the ball in play by a free kick?

85. During a pass play, the quarterback due to pressure commits intentional grounding foul from behind his own goal line. Is the official correct in indicating the penalty is from the spot of the foul toward the end line and results in a safety?
86. During a try-for-point, the right halfback, A1, commits pass interference and the pass is incomplete in the end zone. Is the official correct in indicating no score and no replay?
87. During a pass play, the right offensive end, A1, and a defensive back, B1, who are airborne, simultaneously control a pass over the field of play and come to the ground in B's end zone. Is the official correct in indicating a touchdown?
88. During a free kick, R1 receives the ball on his five-yard line. Because of pressure he runs backward into his own end zone where he is tagged. Is the official correct in indicating a touchback?
89. During a running play from the five-yard line, the right halfback, A1, receives a pitch-out from the quarterback. As he, A1, approaches the goal line his body goes over the goal line but the ball in his possession does not. Is the official correct in indicating a touchdown?
90. During a pass play, a defensive back intercepts in his end zone. He is immediately tagged by the offensive end. Is the official correct in indicating a touchback?

CONDUCT OF PLAYERS AND OTHERS

91. In an attempted block, an offensive halfback has his hand against his body but swings his elbow to strike an opponent. Is the official correct in indicating personal foul, loss of fifteen yards, and disqualification?
92. In an attempted block, an offensive lineman does not have his hands against his body and he uses his forearm to strike an opponent. Is the official correct in indicating illegal use of hands, loss of fifteen yards?
93. After losing fifteen yards on a running play, an offensive halfback slams the ball to the ground. Is the official correct in indicating unsportsmanlike conduct, loss of fifteen yards from the spot of the foul?
94. During a running play to the right, the offensive center and right offensive end go downfield and two-on-one block a defensive halfback. Is the official correct in indicating a personal foul for the illegal two-on-one block?
95. During a pass play, the offensive right end gains a step on a defensive back. Out of desperation, the defensive back pulls the flag of the offensive right end. The pass was incomplete to the offensive right end. Is the official correct in indicating unsportsmanlike conduct, loss of fifteen yards, and disqualification?
96. During a scrimmage kick, a defensive back extends both hands at full arm's length above his head to indicate fair catch signal. The scrimmage kick is caught by his teammate and advanced. Is the official correct in indicating receiving team's ball, first down at the spot of tag?

97. During a running play, the offensive halfback, A2, receives a pitch-out. The quarterback throws a body block with his hand not in contact with his body. Is the official correct in indicating illegal block, loss of fifteen yards?

98. Ball carrier A1 is legally tagged at midfield. After the whistle, a defensive player, B1, clips the right offensive end, A2. A2 then strikes B1. The official indicates fouls by both B1 and A2 but the captain of Team A insults the official for calling the fouls. Is the official correct in indicating three dead-ball fouls that will be administered separately and in the order of occurrence and the offensive right end, A2, will be disqualified?

99. During a running play, the offensive halfback, A2, receives a pitch-out. To gain momentum the quarterback pushes A2 past an opponent. Is the official correct in indicating helping the runner, loss of five yards from spot of foul?

100. During a running play, the offensive left halfback, A3, breaks into the clear. As the defensive halfback, B1, attempts to pull a flag from A3, he blocks with his arms the opportunity for B1 to pull his flag. Is the official correct in indicating personal foul, loss of fifteen yards from spot of foul?

PENALTY ADMINISTRATION AND ENFORCEMENT

101. During a running play, the offensive end is offside A1. After the legal tag, the defensive halfback, B1, commits a personal foul. Is the official correct in administering the penalties separately and in the order of occurrence?

102. During a running play, the offensive halfback goes for a good gain. After the whistle, the offensive center clips an opponent. Is the official correct in measuring the clipping penalty from the spot at which the ball will next be put in play?

103. During a passing play, the offensive right end is offside A1. The quarterback throws an interception to a defensive back, B1. While B1 is advancing the ball, a defensive lineman clips B2, an opponent. Is the official correct in indicating that the offensive offside and the defensive clip constitute a double foul?

104. During a running play, the defensive end, B1, is offside. While the right offensive halfback is carrying the ball, the offensive left end clips A1, an opponent. After the legal tag, the right offensive halfback commits a personal foul on A2. Is the official correct in indicating that the defensive offside B1 and the offensive clip A1 constitute a double foul and down will be replayed? The personal foul on the offensive halfback A2 will be separately administered from the previous spot?

105. During a passing play, the offensive lineman holds A1. The pass is intercepted by a defensive back, B1. While B1 advances the ball, B2 clips an opponent. Is the official correct in indicating that B may retain possession if the penalty for the offensive holding is declined?

106. During a try-for-point, a defensive lineman, B1, is offside and the kick by the offense is good. Is the official correct in indicating to A two options: they may accept the penalty and replay the try, or they may accept the point and have the penalty for the foul by B1 assessed on the succeeding free kick?

107. During a running play, the offensive left halfback, A1, is illegally in motion at the snap. On a sweep to the right, the offensive center, A2, clips a defensive back, and then a legal tag. Is the official correct in measuring these penalties separately and in the order that they were committed?

108. During a running play, the offensive left halfback runs to his own forty-yard line, where he is tagged. During the run there is a holding infraction by the offensive quarterback at his own twenty-yard line. Is the official correct in indicating that the basic spot for enforcement is the spot where the run ended?

109. During a pass play, a defensive back, B1, interferes with the right offensive end, A1. B1 then intercepts the ball. An offensive center then clips A2, an opponent. After the tag the offensive quarterback, A3, commits a personal foul. Is the official correct in indicating that the interference by B1 and the clip by A2 constitute a double foul and the penalties offset? Following the administration of the penalty for the dead-ball foul by A3, the down will be replayed?

110. During a running play, the quarterback scores. Following the touchdown, the offensive left end, A2, strikes a defensive back, B1. During the try-for-point, the offensive right end is offside A3 and a defensive back, B2, interferes in the end zone with A4. Is the official correct in indicating that A2 could be disqualified for his foul and the offside by A3 and pass interference by B2 during the try-for-point results in a double foul and the try-for-point will be replayed? The penalty for the foul by A2 will be administered on the succeeding kickoff.

SCRIMMAGE, SNAPPING, HANDLING, AND PASSING

111. A defensive back uses his hands to ward off a potential receiver prior to the release of the forward pass in flight. Is the official correct in indicating defensive-pass interference?

112. An offensive player (A1) goes out of bounds during a passing play and a defender tips a legal forward pass that is caught by A1 inbounds. Is the official correct in indicating illegal pass reception?

113. During a backward pass play a defender intercepts and runs for a touchdown. Is the official correct in indicating a dead ball at the spot of interception?

114. A player of the offense catches a pass and then fumbles the ball. A player on the defense then catches the fumbled ball before it strikes the ground. Is the official correct in indicating a dead ball at the spot of the fumble?

115. During signals by the quarterback, the defensive linebacker calls his defensive signals while standing in the neutral zone. Is the official correct in *not* calling an infraction?

116. An offensive player charges into the neutral zone but gets back into legal position before the snap. He did not touch or in any way interfere with an opponent. Is the official correct in indicating no penalty?

117. An offensive player who started from his scrimmage line goes in motion. He is two yards behind the line when the ball is snapped. Is the official correct in indicating illegal motion?

118. An umpire indicates offensive pass interference on the ten-yard line. Is he correct in indicating a fifteen-yard penalty from the spot of infraction plus loss of down?

119. The offensive center adjusts the ball before the snap. He then changes the position of the ball and a defensive player charges in at the first sign of movement. Is the official correct in indicating illegal snap by the offense?

120. A referee indicates intentional grounding on the offense. Is the official correct in indicating a five-yard penalty from the previous spot and loss of down?

ANSWER KEY

1. Yes	21. Yes	41. Yes	61. No	81. No	101. Yes
2. Yes	22. Yes	42. Yes	62. No	82. No	102. Yes
3. Yes	23. No	43. Yes	63. No	83. No	103. No
4. Yes	24. No	44. No	64. Yes	84. Yes	104. Yes
5. Yes	25. Yes	45. No	65. Yes	85. Yes	105. Yes
6. No	26. Yes	46. Yes	66. No	86. Yes	106. Yes
7. Yes	27. Yes	47. Yes	67. No	87. Yes	107. No
8. Yes	28. Yes	48. Yes	68. No	88. No	108. No
9. No	29. Yes	49. No	69. Yes	89. No	109. Yes
10. No	30. No	50. No	70. No	90. Yes	110. Yes
11. No	31. Yes	51. Yes	71. No	91. Yes	111. No
12. Yes	32. Yes	52. No	72. No	92. Yes	112. No
13. Yes	33. Yes	53. No	73. No	93. Yes	113. No
14. Yes	34. Yes	54. No	74. Yes	94. Yes	114. No
15. Yes	35. Yes	55. No	75. No	95. Yes	115. No
16. Yes	36. Yes	56. No	76. Yes	96. No	116. Yes
17. No	37. Yes	57. No	77. No	97. No	117. Yes
18. Yes	38. No	58. No	78. No	98. Yes	118. No
19. Yes	39. No	59. Yes	79. Yes	99. Yes	119. Yes
20. Yes	40. Yes	60. No	80. Yes	100. Yes	120. No

7

Summary
of Penalties

The rules, section, and article under the summary of penalties are coded in conjunction with the *Official National Touch and Flag Football Rules* book. The officials' signals with the numbers referring to the numbered illustrations are in the back of this guide in the Officials' Code of Signals section.

SUMMARY OF PENALTIES

Loss of a Down

	RULE	SECTION	ARTICLE	SIGNAL
Illegally handing ball forward (also loss of 5 yards)	7	2	1	13
Illegal forward pass by Team A (also loss of 5 yards)	7	4	2	13
Intentionally grounding pass (also loss of 5 yards)	7	4	2	12
Offensive pass interference (also loss of 15 yards)	7	4	7	14

Loss of 5 Yards

	RULE	SECTION	ARTICLE	SIGNAL
Excess time-out illegally used or requested	3	3	5	6
Illegal delay of game	3	4	2	6
Putting ball in play before declared ready-for-play	3	4	2	2
Infraction of free kick formation	6	1	2	1
Illegal snap	7	1	2	2
Infraction of scrimmage formation	7	1	2	1
Interference with opponents or the ball	7	1	2	2
Offensive player illegally in motion at the snap	7	1	2	3
False start or simulating start of a play	7	1	2	2
Player on line receiving snap	7	1	2	2
Illegally handing ball forward (also loss of down if by Team A)	7	2	1	13
Intentionally grounding pass (also loss of down)	7	4	2	12
Illegal kick	6	3	1	15
Illegal shift	7	1	2	4
Interlocked interference	9	4	3	7
Helping the runner	9	4	1	17

Loss of 15 Yards

<table>
<thead>
<tr><th></th><th>RULE</th><th>SECTION</th><th>ARTICLE</th><th>SIGNAL</th></tr>
</thead>
<tbody>
<tr><td>Team not ready to play at start of either half</td><td>3</td><td>4</td><td>1</td><td>6</td></tr>
<tr><td>Interference with opportunity to catch a kick</td><td>6</td><td>4</td><td>1</td><td>14</td></tr>
<tr><td>Offensive pass interference (also loss of down)</td><td>7</td><td>4</td><td>7</td><td>14</td></tr>
<tr><td>Forward pass illegally touched (also loss of down)</td><td>7</td><td>4</td><td>4</td><td>15</td></tr>
<tr><td>Striking, kicking, kneeing, elbowing, etc</td><td>9</td><td>1</td><td>1</td><td>10</td></tr>
<tr><td>Meeting with knee, striking with open hand, etc</td><td>9</td><td>1</td><td>1</td><td>7</td></tr>
<tr><td>Roughing the kicker or holder</td><td>9</td><td>1</td><td>1</td><td>9</td></tr>
<tr><td>Unsportsmanlike conduct</td><td>9</td><td>1</td><td>2</td><td>10</td></tr>
<tr><td>Infraction of rules during intermissions</td><td>9</td><td>1</td><td>2</td><td>10</td></tr>
<tr><td>Persons illegally on the field</td><td>9</td><td>1</td><td>2</td><td>10</td></tr>
<tr><td>Hurdling</td><td>9</td><td>3</td><td>1</td><td>7</td></tr>
<tr><td>Tripping</td><td>9</td><td>3</td><td>1</td><td>7</td></tr>
<tr><td>Running into opponent obviously out of play</td><td>9</td><td>3</td><td>1</td><td>7</td></tr>
<tr><td>Clipping</td><td>9</td><td>3</td><td>1</td><td>8</td></tr>
<tr><td>Illegal use of hand or arm by offense</td><td>9</td><td>4</td><td>2</td><td>11</td></tr>
<tr><td>Illegal use of hand or arm by defense</td><td>9</td><td>3</td><td>1</td><td>11</td></tr>
<tr><td>Protecting flags</td><td>9</td><td>4</td><td>5</td><td>7</td></tr>
</tbody>
</table>

Offended Team's Ball at Spot of Foul

<table>
<thead>
<tr><th></th><th>RULE</th><th>SECTION</th><th>ARTICLE</th><th>SIGNAL</th></tr>
</thead>
<tbody>
<tr><td>Short free kick illegally touched by kicking team</td><td>6</td><td>1</td><td>4</td><td>2</td></tr>
<tr><td>Illegally touching free kick after being out of bounds</td><td>6</td><td>1</td><td>4</td><td>2</td></tr>
<tr><td>Defensive pass interference</td><td>7</td><td>4</td><td>7</td><td>14</td></tr>
<tr><td>Illegal use of hand or arm when ball is free</td><td>9</td><td>3</td><td>1</td><td>11</td></tr>
<tr><td>Illegally batting free ball</td><td>9</td><td>5</td><td>1</td><td>15</td></tr>
<tr><td>Illegally kicking or kicking at a free ball</td><td>9</td><td>5</td><td>2</td><td>15</td></tr>
<tr><td>Other fouls when the ball is free</td><td>10</td><td>2</td><td>1</td><td>-</td></tr>
</tbody>
</table>

Violation

<table>
<thead>
<tr><th></th><th>RULE</th><th>SECTION</th><th>ARTICLE</th><th>SIGNAL</th></tr>
</thead>
<tbody>
<tr><td>Illegal touching of free kick by kicking team (offended team's ball at spot)</td><td>6</td><td>1</td><td>4</td><td>15</td></tr>
<tr><td>Illegal touching of scrimmage kick</td><td>6</td><td>3</td><td>5</td><td>15</td></tr>
</tbody>
</table>

8

Official Code
of Signals

1. Offside: Infraction of scrimmage or free-kick formation. Penalty: five yards.
Hands on hips.

2. Illegal procedure, position, or substitution: This indicates several different infractions, the more common being: false start; encroachment; having less than the correct number of players on the offensive team's scrimmage line; illegal snap; infraction of substitution rules. Penalty: five yards.

Palms of hands facing chest followed by over and over rotation motion.

3. Illegal motion: Player or players illegally in motion when the ball is snapped. Penalty: five yards.

Horizontal arc with either hand.

4. Illegal Shift: Player or players failed to stop for one second after a shift. Penalty: five yards.
Horizontal arc with both hands.

5. Start the clock or no more timeouts allowed.
Full arm circle to simulate winding clock.

6. Delay of game: Excess time-outs requested or used; illegal delay of game; team not ready to play. Penalty: five or fifteen yards.
Folded arms

7. Personal foul: Striking, kicking, or kneeing an opponent; hurdling; tripping; running into opponent out of play. Penalty: fifteen yards.
Arm outstretched, palm down; movement up and down.

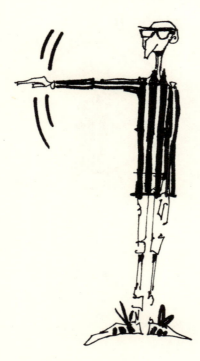

8. Clipping: A foul committed when a player attempts to block from behind by throwing himself across the back or legs of an opponent other than the runner. Penalty: fifteen yards.
Striking back of calf with hand.

9. Roughing the kicker: The kicker, or the holder of the ball for the placekick, has been run into or otherwise illegally interfered with. Penalty: fifteen yards.
Lifting of leg in kicking motion.

10. Unsportsmanlike conduct: Besides general unsportsmanlike conduct by a player, the signal also indicates: persons illegally on the field; deliberate or flagrant acts such as kneeing, kicking, and if flagrant, offender shall be disqualified. Penalty: fifteen yards.
Arms outstretched, palms down.

11. Illegal use of hands and arms: Penalty: fifteen yards from spot of foul.
Grasping of one wrist at chest level.

12. Intentional grounding: Penalty: five yards and loss of down.
Hands raised in front of chest with palms facing each other followed by down motion.

13. Illegally passing or handing ball forward: Penalty: five yards and loss of down.
Hand behind back.

14. Forward pass or kick catching interference: Offensive pass interference: fifteen yards and loss of down penalty. Defensive pass interference: pass ruled complete at spot of foul, first down. Interference with opportunity to catch a kick: fifteen-yard penalty beyond spot of foul, first down.
Push hands forward from shoulder with hands vertical.

15. Ball illegally touched, kicked, or batted: Deliberately kicking a free ball, a pass, or a ball being held for a place-kick by an opponent. If a ball is free, offended team's ball at spot of foul. If in possession, it is fifteen yards from the previous spot.
Tapping both shoulders with fingertips.

16. Incomplete forward pass, penalty declined, no play, or no score: *Shifting of hands in horizontal plane.*

17. Helping the runner, or interlocked interference: Penalty: five yards from the spot of foul.
Pushing movement of hands to front with arms downward.

18. Ball dead: If hand is moved from side to side, touchback.
One arm aloft, open hand.

19. Touchdown or field goal:
Both arms extended above head.

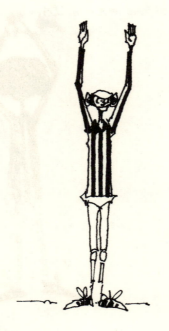

20. Safety:
Palms together over head.

21. Time-out:
Hands crisscrossed over head.

22. First down:
Arm raised, then pointed toward defensive team's goal.

23. Ball ready for play:
Arm extended above, movement up and down.

24. Loss of down:
Both hands placed behind neck.

Bibliography

Clegg, Richard and William Thompson. *Modern Sports Officiating*. Dubuque, Iowa: William C. Brown Company, 1974.

National Alliance Football Committee. *1973 Football Officials' Manual*. Chicago: National Federation of State High School Athletic Associations, 1973.

National Football League. *Officials' Manual For Professional Football*. New York, New York. 1973.

The National Touch and Flag Football Committee. *The National Touch and Flag Football Rules*. Chicago: The Athletic Institute, 1971.

Index

Backward pass, 145; recovery of, 147
Ball dead, signal of, 180
Ball illegally touched, kicked, or batted, signal of, 178
Ball ready for play, signal of, 182
Batting free ball, illegally, 170
Blocking, 131–33, 136

Clipping, 170; signal of, 175
Clock starts, 101–2, 106
Clock stops, 101, 107
Conduct of players, 130, 169; flagrant fouls, 130, 134, 140, 169; personal foul, 130, 135, 139, 136–42, 169; unsportsmanlike conduct, 130, 138, 140, 169

Dead ball, 116, 117, 120, 121
Delay of game, 104, 169, 170; signal of, 174
Down, 116; first, 116, 119; series of, 116

Equipment, 16–17

Field goal, 110, 114
First down, signal of, 182
Forward pass, 169; complete, 118, 147; illegal, 143, 146–47, 169; interference during, 144, 148–49, 169, 170; legal, 144, 146
Free kick, 122, 143, 169; fair catch of, 123, 130; first touching of, 122, 128, 170; recovery of, 122; restraining line, 122, 123; out-of-bounds, 126–29

Game time, 101–2

Handling, 143, 169; illegal, 169
Helping the runner, signal of, 179
Hurdling, 134, 169

Illegal motion, signal of, 172
Illegal pass, signal of, 177
Illegal procedure, signal of, 172
Illegal shift, signal of, 173
Illegal use of hands, signal of, 176
Incomplete forward pass, signal of, 179
Intentional grounding, signal of, 177
Intentionally grounding pass, 169

Kicking at free ball, illegally, 170

Linesman, 13–14; duties, end of game, 79–80, 100; field goal position and duty of, 58–61, 94–95; general position, responsibilities of, 32–33; goal-line plays, position and duty of, 61–65, 96–97; kickoff position and duty of, 35–38, 80–83; penalty administration, 68–71, 75, 99–100; pregame duties of, 25; scrimmage kick position and duty of, 53–57, 91–93; scrimmage pass position and duty of, 46–52, 88–90; scrimmage run position and duty of, 40–44, 84–87; timeout, 66–67, 98–99; try-for-point position and duty of, 58–61, 94–95
Live ball, 116, 120, 143
Loss of down, signal of, 182

Official National Touch and Flag Football Rules, 30, 101, 169
Officiating procedure, knowledge of, 15
Offside, signal of, 171
Out-of-bounds, 111, 116, 119, 122

Pass or kick interference, signal of, 178

Penalties, 149; dead-ball foul, enforcement of, 149, 150, 151, 155, 157, 158; double foul, enforcement of, 149, 151, 154; enforcement spots of, basic, 150, 154, 155, 156; enforcement spots of, special, 152, 158; multiple foul, enforcement of, 149, 150, 151; replay of, 151, 153

Personal foul, signal of, 174

Protecting flags, 139, 170

Ready for play, 66, 98, 169

Referee, 13–14; coin toss duties of, 27–29; end of game, 79–80, 100; field goal position and duty of, 58–61, 94–95; general position responsibilities of, 31, 33; goal-line plays position and duty of, 61–65, 96–97; kickoff position and duty of, 35–37, 80–83; penalty administration, 68–80, 99–100; pregame duties of, 25; pregame responsibility of, 24; ready for play, 66, 98; scrimmage kick position and duty, 53–57, 91, 93; scrimmage pass position and duty of, 46–52, 88–90; scrimmage run position and duty of, 40–43, 84–87; time-out, 66–67, 98–99; try-for-point position and duty of, 58–61, 94–95

Roughing the kicker, signal of, 175

Rules, knowledge of, 14

Safety, 110, 113, 114, 152; signal of, 181

Scrimmage, 143, 144, 146, 169

Scrimmage kick, 122; fair catch, 123, 130; first touching of, 122, 124, 170; out-of-bounds, 125; protection of, 122, 124; recovery of, 122, 125, 129, 170

Self-analysis, 159–68

Signals, 16, 171–82

Snap, 143; false start, 152, 169; illegal, 169; illegal motion, 169; motion at, 146; shift, 170

Start clock, signal of, 173

Substitution, 102, 109

Three-man officiating crew, 13, 31–33, 160–61 (see also Referee, Linesman, Umpire)

Time-Out, 102; charged, 102–6; illegal, 169; officials, 107–8; signal of, 181

Touchback, 110, 115

Touchdown, 110, 111, 112

Touchdown or field goal, signal of, 180

Tripping, 170

Two-man officiating crew, 14, 33, 161 (see also Referee, Linesman)

Umpire, 13–14; end of game duties of, 79–80; field goal position and duty of, 58–61; general position responsibilities of, 32; goal-line plays position and duty of, 61–65; kickoff position and duty of, 35–39; penalty administration, 68–71, 76; pregame duties of, 26–27; scrimmage kick position and duty of, 53–57; scrimmage pass position and duty of, 46–52; scrimmage run position and duty of, 40–45; time-out, 66–67; try-for-point position and duty of, 58–61

Unsportsmanlike conduct, signal of, 176

Use of hands illegally, 133, 170

Whistle, sounding of, 17–20